THE ONCE AND FUTURE SECURITY COUNCIL

THE ONCE AND FUTURE SECURITY COUNCIL

Edited by Bruce Russett

with contributions by

Ian Hurd
Soo Yeon Kim
Barry O'Neill
James S. Sutterlin
Masayuki Tadokoro
Nigel Thalakada

St. Martin's Press
New York

THE ONCE AND FUTURE SECURITY COUNCIL
Copyright © Bruce Russett, 1997. All rights reserved. Printed in the United States of America. No part of this book may be used or reproduced in any manner whatsoever without written permission except in the case of brief quotations embodied in critical articles or reviews. For information, address St. Martin's Press, 175 Fifth Avenue, New York, N.Y. 10010.

ISBN 0-312-16556-0

Table 3.4, page 50, reprinted from *The United Nations: International Organization and World Politics,* Second Edition, by Robert E. Riggs and Jack C. Plano, copyright © 1994 by Harcourt Brace & Company. Reproduced by permission of the publisher.

Library of Congress Cataloging-in-Publication Data

The once and future security council / Bruce Russett, [editor].
    p. cm.
  Includes bibliographical references and index.
  ISBN 0-312-16556-0
  1. United Nations. Security Council. 2. United Nations. Security Council—Rules and practice. 3. United Nations. Security Council—Voting. I. Russett, Bruce M.
JX1977.O56   1997
341.23'23—DC20   96-34854
                                                                              CIP

Design by Acme Art, Inc.

First edition: March 1997
10 9 8 7 6 5 4 3 2 1

CONTENTS

Preface vii

Chapter One: The Past as Prologue 1
    James S. Sutterlin

Chapter Two: Ten Balances for Weighing UN Reform Proposals 13
    Bruce Russett

Chapter Three: The New Politics of Voting Alignments in the
    General Assembly 29
    Soo Yeon Kim and Bruce Russett

Chapter Four: Power and Satisfaction in the Security Council 59
    Barry O'Neill

Chapter Five: China's Voting Pattern in the
    Security Council, 1990–1995 83
    Nigel Thalakada

Chapter Six: A Japanese View on Restructuring the
    Security Council 119
    Masayuki Tadokoro

Chapter Seven: Security Council Reform:
    Informal Membership and Practice 135
    Ian Hurd

Chapter Eight: Breaking the Restructuring Logjam 153
    Bruce Russett, Barry O'Neill, and James S. Sutterlin

Contributors 173

Index 175

PREFACE

This book stems from a two-year project, centered at the program in United Nations Studies at Yale University, to understand the possibilities for changing the composition and procedures of the United Nations Security Council, and the difficulties in making such changes. Proposals for revision have emerged with increased urgency in recent years. Driving these proposals is a widespread recognition that the Security Council is now more able than it was during the Cold War years to reach agreement to authorize peacekeeping and peace enforcement missions. Yet at the same time, the composition of the Security Council has been little changed since its creation in 1945. Most importantly, the original five permanent members retain by far the greatest share of voting power due to their right to veto resolutions and other substantive actions—but this power is not proportionate to the configuration of power and influence of states in international relations more generally.

Demands arise to reconfigure Council membership so as better to represent states' wider power and the differing interests of the full membership of the United Nations. It is far from clear, however, precisely what configuration would be broadly regarded as representative, and hence would contribute to preserving the legitimacy of the Security Council as an institution. Nor can one find agreement about how best to preserve the ability of the Council to act in a timely and effective manner, nor about the best balance of possible trade-offs between representativeness and effectiveness. Nor, even if substantial agreement could be reached on these questions, is it clear if that agreement could be sufficient actually to bring the necessary legal and political changes into being. In putting together this book we have analyzed these problems in the light of historical experience and using various analytical techniques to elucidate the underlying constraints.

James Sutterlin opens the volume with a review of the founding of the United Nations, and the efforts of the founders to shape this new organ of international security in ways that would avoid the limitations of its preceding institution, the League of Nations. In doing so he shows, with a strong sense of déjà vu, how the arguments and proposals of most member states then presaged very similar arguments and proposals in the current debate. The fundamental interests of powerful states, and of weak ones—and their competing efforts to control the organization—have not changed very much. Then, as now, debates considered the number of states to be on the Council, the length of their terms, the voting rules by which decisions would be reached, and the degree of openness in procedure and debate that would shape those decisions.

In the next chapter, Bruce Russett sets forth ten "balances" or dialectical opposites useful for evaluating any proposal or set of proposals for United Nations reform. While these balances apply fully to the wide discourse of reform pertaining to all organs and agencies of the United Nations, some are especially applicable to the debate about the future of the Security Council, which is embedded in that wider debate. They include balances between the preservation of state sovereignty and the erosion of sovereignty in the interest of human security, between the demands of power and of justice, and between vision and practicality. Changes to the Security Council will necessarily be part of a much wider agenda for change, reflecting these and other balances in any political agreement among the UN's varied membership.

In the third chapter, Soo Yeon Kim and Bruce Russett empirically identify change and continuity in the voting alignments of states in the General Assembly and in the kinds of issues that underlie the voting alignments. They do so as a way to estimate some of the divisions and positions of states that also characterize much of the business before the Security Council, but which are harder to identify in that body, where contested votes are much less common. For the first 45 years of the United Nations, states voted in a way that can be characterized in familiar geopolitical terms by an East-West axis and a North-South one, with the former defined primarily by the Cold War rivalry and the latter principally by the division between rich industrialized states and poor ones, most of whom were former colonies of some of the rich countries. During these years the East-West division was the more dominant. But the end of the Cold War brought the dissolution of the Soviet-led coalition that anchored the Eastern end of that axis and the shift of most of the former Warsaw Pact countries and successor states onto the Western side. Now the North-South division—cast in terms reflecting concerns not just for military security but more broadly with "human security"—dominates General Assembly voting, with residual elements of the East-West split only one-fourth as prominent. This division between rich and poor also underlies the debates and the decisions of the Security Council.

The next chapter, by Barry O'Neill, develops a rigorous method for measuring the relative power that member states are able to exercise in the Security Council. That power derives from the veto power that resides in the status of permanent member and from the rules establishing a "supermajority" (more than one-half of the members) by which resolutions must be approved. Essentially he shows that the voting power of each permanent member is many times that of even all the nonpermanent members together, and that in any addition of new members to the Council that disproportion would not materially change. Membership without a veto gives now, and would give, very little voting power. Even among permanent members, however, actual power over outcomes varies substantially according to the configuration of members on the major issue dimensions. The veto is most critical to the permanent member—currently China—that is most "distant" from the center of gravity of other states' issue positions. O'Neill also shows, however, that states without much voting power, or even not members of the Council at all, may nonetheless be quite satisfied with the outcome of voting if their allies have power. Germany and Italy, not permanent members of the Council now, have had little formal power but by O'Neill's measure appear quite satisfied with the actual decisions taken.

The next two chapters examine the experience and perspectives of two states that occupy especially critical positions in the restructuring discussion. The first is China, which because of its relative political isolation on some issues before the Security Council arguably benefits most from the veto power accorded to a permanent member of the Council. Some of the special leverage it is currently able to exert would be diluted if one or more other less-developed countries should become permanent members with vetoes. The second state deserving special attention is Japan, which has probably campaigned most insistently for a permanent seat on the Council. In many ways its political alignment and arguments for achieving permanent membership also apply to Germany's desire for similar status.

In chapter five, Nigel Thalakada takes a detailed look at the voting behavior of China on the Council in recent years. He shows that whereas China has not cast any vetoes during this period, it has frequently abstained or expressed reservations even while voting with the majority. China has typically utilized abstentions on votes authorizing the use of coercive power under the principles of Chapter VII of the United Nations Charter, or on resolutions that the Chinese government regarded as intrusions into the domestic affairs of a sovereign state. Moreover, China has been able to utilize the implicit or explicit threat of casting a veto either to modify a resolution or to extract side payments on issues, such as trade or charges of human rights violations, important to the Chinese government. In doing so Thalakada documents in practice the power a veto conveys in O'Neill's theoretical analysis.

In the next chapter, Masayuki Tadokoro addresses several requirements for any adequate restructuring. One is the need to mobilize greater resources for the UN, including in the fields of economic and social activities important to peacebuilding. Others are the demands of efficiency, legitimacy, and political feasibility. To meet these requirements he suggests the possibility of moving to a weighted voting system, rather like that used in the IMF, that would effectively retain the veto power of existing permanent members and implicitly give such a veto to most new permanent members. He argues that some reform that brings Japan into the Council is important to building a constructive engagement by Japan in world political affairs.

In chapter seven, recognizing the difficulty and perhaps impossibility of formal change in the structure of the Security Council in the near term, Ian Hurd asks whether formal change is really so essential. He applies organization theory to discuss how institutions characterized as "open systems" must adapt to environmental change, but often can do so informally in circumstances when formal change is not possible. In doing so, Hurd considers the ways in which Germany and Japan have come to be consulted on the major financial commitments entailed in major peacekeeping operations, and similarly the process by which troop-contributing countries are brought into decision making whether or not they happen to be members of the Council. He also looks at the development of consultation among the states of the large Non-Aligned Movement and the ways in which they try to increase unity among those of their members who at any particular time are on the Security Council in a nonpermanent capacity. He then discusses some of the current possibilities for informal adaptation, and the degree to which these can or cannot plausibly substitute for formal change.

Finally, Russett, O'Neill, and Sutterlin bring together many of these analytical and empirical threads to identify the constraints and opportunities offered by various kinds of proposals to modify the composition or procedures of the Security Council. They conclude that so long as the veto power remains intact, no addition of new members without the veto will much change the basic distribution of power on the Council. And, by their understanding, abolition of the veto is really impossible to imagine, and the addition of new permanent members with a veto is very unlikely given the high hurdles posed by the rules for Charter amendment. But voting power is not everything. They suggest that a package of changes, with some at least symbolic gain for nearly every state, might both be achievable and protect the Council's ability to act effectively and legitimately in the eyes of the world at large. This package would include expanding the number of nonpermanent members, permitting a nonpermanent member to be reelected immediately without missing a term, and slightly raising the proportion of affirmative votes required to pass a resolution, thus somewhat strengthening the hands of nonpermanent members, who can band together in a bloc. Other pieces of the package might include some narrowing of the scope of issues to which a veto may apply, deleting the anachronistic Charter references to "enemy states," and broadening the Council's procedures for consultation and transparency in decision making.

• • •

For support of the research and discussions underpinning this project we are indebted to three foundations: the Ford Foundation, which underwrote work of the Yale Secretariat that helped prepare the Report of the Independent Working Group on the Future of the United Nations; and the Carnegie Corporation of New York and the Center for Global Partnership of the Japan Foundation, both of which supported our work independent of and following that of the Working Group. We discussed the ideas and tentative conclusions at a number of meetings with the staff of countries' UN missions in New York and with staff of the UN Secretariat. An international meeting hosted by the East-West Center in Hawaii was crucial to evaluating these ideas and bringing them together in a focused form; four of the chapters were developed from papers at that workshop. We are especially grateful to the participants in that meeting, and chapter eight represents an effort to distill and synthesize many of those deliberations. Our colleagues at Yale, including President Richard Levin, Paul Kennedy of Yale's program in International

Security Studies, and Gaddis Smith of the Center for International and Area Studies, helped make United Nations Studies at Yale a unit capable of pursuing this project. Of course none of these individuals, groups, or foundations is responsible for or necessarily would agree with our conclusions, and we expand and modify some elements of the Working Group's Report. We also are grateful to all of our faculty colleagues and graduate students whose discussions helped shape our thinking and stimulate our creativity. Karen Yoder serves, effectively and tempered by good humor, as administrator of UNSY.

Some contributions to this volume are revised and expanded versions of journal articles published previously, and used with permission of the publishers. Specifically, an earlier version of chapter two appeared in *Political Science Quarterly*, Volume 111, Number 2 (Summer 1996), copyright 1996 by the American Academy of Political Science; of chapter three in *International Organization,* Volume 50, Number 3 (Autumn 1966), copyright 1966 by Massachusetts Institute of Technology Press; of chapter four in *Journal of Conflict Resolution*, Volume 40, Number 2 (June 1996), copyright 1996 by Sage Publications, Inc.; and of chapter eight in *Global Governance: A Review of Multilateralism and International Organizations,* Volume 2, Number 1 (January-April 1996), copyright 1996 by Lynne Riener Publishers, Inc.

Bruce Russett
New Haven, Connecticut
October 1996

1

THE PAST AS PROLOGUE

JAMES S. SUTTERLIN

At its 47th session, the United Nations General Assembly adopted a resolution (47/62) requesting the Secretary-General to invite member states to submit written comments on a possible review of the membership of the Security Council and to incorporate these comments in a report to the next session of the Assembly. More than 100 states have provided their views. They range well beyond the question of membership and vary so much in detail as almost to defy structured analysis. Yet, when considered under a number of broad headings, it emerges that, to a striking degree, the proposals for change made now are remarkably similar in intent to suggestions put forward 50 years ago at the founding conference of the UN at San Francisco. At that time most of the changes suggested in the draft that was before the conference did not gain acceptance. Similarly, the General Assembly Working Group established to consider the views of member states and formulate recommendations regarding the structure of the Security Council has been unable until now to reach agreement on the central issues involved.

At San Francisco the delegations had before them the detailed proposals for the structure and functions of the Security Council that had been agreed by the Soviet Union, the United Kingdom, and the United States at Dumbarton Oaks and at Yalta (and separately by China). Like the member states today, the delegations at San Francisco did not seriously challenge the central concept of the Security Council. They did not object to its mandate to take decisions on behalf of the membership in matters of peace and security nor to the requirement that members comply with the decisions of the Council for action under Chapter VII of the Charter. There was no quarrel with the concept of enforcement measures. The principal objections and suggested amendments related to the size of the Council, the representative (or nonrepresentative) nature of the membership, the relationship of the Council to the General Assembly and to regional organizations, and, of course, to the veto right accorded only to the five permanent members. By and large, these are the same concerns expressed by members today. Notably, neither then nor now, were there more than a few suggestions that the veto power itself be abolished.

The widespread current examination of the structure of the Security Council was encouraged by the fiftieth anniversary of the United Nations, seen by many as a potential catalytic deadline for bringing significant change to the Organization. While the anniversary passed without bringing agreement on reform, consideration of the possible enlargement of the Council has continued in the Working Group, spurred by the insistent efforts of Japan and Germany to obtain a permanent seat and, equally, by the long-standing discontent of many member states with the unrepresentative nature of Council membership. In this context, it can be useful to look back and examine the reasons why the three major wartime allies (with the United States taking the lead) shaped the Council as they did, have resisted—together with their French and Chinese colleagues—most changes since, and may well continue to do so unless the proposed changes are quite limited in their effect.

The Legacy of the League

The League of Nations was seen by the planners of the UN as an example both of what could usefully be emulated and what should by all means be avoided. The latter was the controlling consideration in the case of the Security Council. Three serious weaknesses in the organization of the League were viewed as adversely affecting its capacity to maintain peace: (1) the rule of consensus made it difficult to take decisions;[1] (2) the lack of differentiation between the Assembly and the Council in dealing with security questions caused confusion and delays and led to inaction; and (3) the provisions in the League Covenant for enforcement measures were inadequate and ineffective, at least as interpreted by the membership.

To avoid these problems, majority voting was provided for the Council—qualified, of course, by the veto right. A clear distinction was drawn between the Security Council and the General Assembly, with the former alone mandated to *take action* on behalf of international security. The General Assembly could discuss any matter relating to international peace and security and could make recommendations to the Council except when the Security Council had the matter under consideration, unless the Council requested such. Further, Chapter VII of the Charter authorized the Council to impose, and required the membership to comply with, firm enforcement measures.

The special role accorded the five permanent members was heavily influenced by the wartime experience of the Allies. In his final report to President Truman on the San Francisco Conference, Secretary of State Stettinius wrote: "It was taken as axiomatic at Dumbarton Oaks, and continued to be the view of the Sponsoring Powers at San Francisco, that the cornerstone for world security is the unity of those nations which formed the core of the grand alliance against the Axis." This led to the conclusion that a general security system should be adopted based on (1) the principle of sovereign equality of all peace-loving states and (2) the predominant responsibility of the great powers in matters relating to peace and security.[2] It automatically flowed from this conclusion that the key to the effectiveness of the UN in the maintenance of international security would be the unity of the great powers as permanent members of the Security Council. This concept corresponded with President Roosevelt's idea of the "four policemen" who would be principally responsible for maintaining peace and dealing with aggression.

It was assumed in the planning undertaken by the United States for the new international organization, and in the subsequent discussions in Dumbarton Oaks and San Francisco, that the major powers would provide most of the troops and equipment for enforcement actions under Chapter VII. The Americans realized that the U.S. Senate would never ratify the UN Charter unless the United States retained clear control of the utilization of American military force. (It had turned down the League Covenant partly from fear that American soldiers would be automatically called for duty contrary to United States interests.) In the different context of today, when the United States is, after many years, providing troops and equipment for military operations authorized or undertaken by the UN, this reasoning has regained evident relevance, as shown in the opposition persistently expressed in Congress to the deployment and command of American troops by the UN. Realizing that it would be in a minority position in the world organization, the USSR supported (too wholeheartedly, it turned out) the veto principle. Winston Churchill, after initial hesitation, also agreed.

There was strong resistance to the veto privilege of the permanent members at San Francisco. The Latin Americans were especially critical, since they feared that a non-American power could veto Security Council authorization for action by the Latin American regional organization to deal with a threat to peace in the Hemisphere. The United States and the USSR made clear, however, that the veto was the price of their participation. That settled the matter.

There were numerous complaints that a Security Council of 11 members (as it was until 1965), 5 of them permanent, would be unrepresentative, undemocratic, and arbitrary. Various amendments were submitted at San Francisco to increase the size of the Security Council, usually by adding 3 or 4 elected members. The Latin Americans made a strong effort to obtain either a permanent seat for the region or at least a definite allocation of nonpermanent ones. Three seats out of some larger membership was frequently suggested for assignment to the Western Hemisphere (in addition to the U.S. seat). Liberia proposed an alphabetical rotation of nonpermanent members to guarantee the participation of all states.

In response, the sponsoring powers argued that democracy was preserved since the permanent members could not adopt a resolution without two votes of nonpermanent members, the necessary majority being seven. Moreover, the provision that a member could not be elected to a second successive term assured that there would be wide representation over time. The most forceful argument, however, and one that retains its resonance today, was that to be an effective body in dealing with threats to peace, the Council had to be small and capable of quick decisions. When a number of medium-sized countries contended that *even* a Council of 15 members could be effective, the sponsoring powers demurred.

Medium powers such as Belgium and Australia were particularly persistent in their criticism, since they felt that they could and would be expected to make a substantial contribution to the maintenance of international security. France, Canada, and Australia proposed that the criteria for nonpermanent membership include the ability and willingness to contribute to international security. India suggested that due regard should be paid to population and economic capacity in selecting nonpermanent members. Australia wanted nonpermanent members to be immediately eligible for reelection, an idea that is now on the list of proposals being considered by the General Assembly Working Group.

In reply to such views and to answer complaints on the nonrepresentative nature of the Council, an amendment was accepted providing that in the election of nonpermanent members, due regard would be paid (1) "in the first instance" to the contribution of members to the maintenance of international peace and security and to the other purposes of the Organization, and (2) to equitable geographic distribution. The first of these criteria was soon ignored in favor of the second, but it now figures in the discussion of criteria for additional permanent members.

One addition to the Dumbarton Oaks proposals is worth particular attention in the context of the present greatly expanded use of military force by the United Nations. The present Article 44 was accepted in response to a Canadian complaint that there should be no taxation without representation, meaning, in the case of the Security Council, that a nonmember of the Council who contributes troops for enforcement action should have a say in how they are utilized. This article[3] has understandably received little attention since it has never been used. Yet, it provides the only opening for a nonmember of the Council to join in the debate, and, according to the legislative history, actually vote on a measure. It would seem to offer a precedent that could have been, and might still be, built upon to expand the Council for decisions on designated subjects.

The Role of the General Assembly in Security Matters

When by the time of the Korean War the Security Council was clearly immobilized by the lack of unity among the permanent members, the United States turned to one of the ideas it had earlier rejected at San Francisco (and that in a different form is again being suggested by a number of member states): giving the General Assembly a greater voice in security questions. The American answer was the Uniting For Peace resolution, under which a security issue can be transferred to the General Assembly *for action* in the event action is blocked in the Council by a veto. While the resolution seems to have departed from the intent of the Charter by authorizing the Assembly to take action on security matters, it did not transfer to the Assembly the unique authority of the Council to make decisions with which members are required to comply: Under the resolution, the Assembly may only recommend or call for action. For this reason it was only moderately effective in strengthening pursuit of victory in the Korean War. Since then, however, the resolution has proved valuable and may suggest how the General Assembly may play a larger role in the maintenance of international security as international security is increasingly understood to mean the security of people as well as states.

Four cases illustrate how the General Assembly can usefully work with the Security Council, or replace it if necessary, in dealing with this aspect of international security.

1. The Assembly authorized the first true peacekeeping operation, UNEF I, in the Sinai.
2. When action on the Soviet invasion of Afghanistan was blocked in the Security Council, the General Assembly "called for" the withdrawal of all foreign troops. This had no effect. But the Assembly also called for UN assistance to the Afghan refugees who had fled to neighboring countries. This provided the basis, or legitimacy, for the huge program carried out to assist more than three million refugees.
3. When it became clear that the Security Council would not authorize a mission to monitor and help provide security for elections in Haiti in 1990 (when Jean-Bertrand Aristide was elected), the General Assembly adopted a resolution authorizing such a mission, although it could not agree to provide funds for it.
4. The General Assembly has assumed a degree of responsibility for strengthening democracy by establishing within the Secretariat the Electoral Assistance Division, which is mandated to assist countries in holding free elections.

In drawing conclusions from these cases it must first be acknowledged that, in the now accepted view, only the Security Council may authorize military peacekeeping operations. The precedent of UNEF I can nonetheless be useful if, as has been suggested,[4] the General Assembly is given (or simply assumes) a major role in dealing with threats to international security when the threat stems from causes within the Assembly's acknowledged field of competence, e.g., social and economic development, humanitarian assistance, protection of human rights and, by extrapolation, the strengthening of democratic institutions. "Peacekeeping" operations intended to alleviate such threats may be predominantly civilian or may not include military personnel at all.

The point is simply this: In the face of the threats to security that are likely to dominate the post–Cold War era, there is justification—and need—for the General Assembly to have a greater role in the maintenance of peace, to work more closely with the Security Council, and to share some of its responsibility. It is one of the ironies of history that such changes would be in line with the suggestions made in 1945 under quite different circumstances.

The "qualified veto," first proposed, as noted earlier, at the San Francisco Conference, is another idea that in the post–Cold War era could offer a way of answering demands for greater democracy and less domination by the permanent members. The veto was conceived primarily as a means of protecting the security interests of those powers that would bear the greatest responsibility in ensuring peace through the use of their military strength. It has surely been a misuse of this power to prevent action that had no real relevance to security, such as the blocking of UN membership simply because a country was allied with one of the permanent members and hostile to another. This fortunately is now a matter of history, but the veto has recently been used (one of only three times in six years, twice by Russia) to prevent a change in the way a peacekeeping operation is financed—hardly a real security issue. The United States vetoed a resolution critical of a friendly state (Israel) when such criticism could, in itself, hardly pose a threat to global security or the security of the United States. It would be a radical step, but one quite in line with the original justification of the veto, if its application were limited to proposed action under Chapter VII of the Charter, or, if that were too restrictive in light of the expanding definition of peacekeeping, limited to action under Chapter VII and any other action involving the use of military force. Among other advantages, this would have the democratizing effect of excluding the selection of the Secretary-General from the veto.

Procedure and Transparency

Despite the political battles in which it has been frequently involved and the hostility that has existed for extended periods between member governments, the Security Council has functioned for almost half a century with remarkable procedural stability. Almost all the current rules of procedure were adopted "provisionally" in 1946. They have gained the permanence of which only the provisional is capable. The sole rule that caused heated conflict when it was first considered provided for the holding of private meetings. Australia fought a bitter fight against it, in which it was joined by a number of other medium-sized countries, on the ground that this would be a reversion to the secret diplomacy that had led to the First World War. Australia was defeated in the Council by a vote of ten to one. Private meetings, which are restricted to Council members, have been held over the years largely for a limited number of sensitive subjects, such as deciding on the Council's choice for Secretary-General, although recently meetings of an even more restricted nature have been limited to the Permanent Representatives, with no assistants or Secretariat staff present. The only structural change in the Council has been the increase, voted in 1963 and ratified in 1965, of the number of its members from 11 to the current 15. The increase was entirely in the number of nonpermanent members and was intended to enhance the representative nature of the Council.

There has, however, been one gradual change in the practice of the Council, governed neither by the Charter nor the Rules of Procedure, which has been of real importance—for good or for bad depending on one's perspective. This is the practice of informal consultations. In the early days, Council members found it useful to gather together in the crowded office of the Council President to discuss, without benefit of interpreters or note takers, how to handle current issues, including the language of resolutions. Such off-the-record, "non-committing" exchanges were very helpful in working out agreements on substantive as well as procedural matters. There was no need for the rhetoric and posturing that had become a part of the public Security Council meetings, which often produced more drama than progress.

By the beginning of the 1970s the consultations had become more frequent, more crowded, and more in need of orderly procedure. Seeing the need, the Federal Republic of Germany donated a commodious consultation room adjacent to the Security Council Chamber, replete with simultaneous translation facilities. Each ambassador could now bring along more assistants, and there was also room for a fair number of Secretariat personnel. The consultations became a small replica of the regular Council meetings except that the proceedings were confidential, attendance was limited to Council members and the Secretariat, and no official notes were taken. Most important decisions are now developed in this consultative, "behind the doors" process. In the formal meetings, with the outcome largely predetermined, speeches are made for the record and votes are officially recorded.

This practice has unquestionably facilitated the process of compromise and agreement among Council members. It has become an established part of the decision-making process. In reality, what goes on in the consultations is seldom kept secret for very long. The representatives attending usually brief their regional groups, and selected press representatives as well, on the proceedings almost immediately. Still, the sense of exclusion is strong and has led, especially among the small countries that rarely have an opportunity to serve as members, to antipathy and distrust toward the Council. As a result, the habit of informal consultations has intensified the call for enlarging the Council. There have been more proposals on enlargement than on any other subject in the comments submitted by member states to the Secretary-General for inclusion in his report to the General Assembly.

What Needs to Change?

The Security Council, which remains essentially as devised half a century ago, is functioning efficiently—more efficiently than ever before in its history. Such weaknesses as have been evident in its functioning in the past two or three years have derived not from its unrepresentative composition or from the use of the veto but rather from: (1) its inadequate capacity to ensure the proper execution of its decisions; (2) its inadequate access to resources for peacekeeping and its inability to bring together the various resources available elsewhere in the system for the objectives of conflict prevention and peace-building; and (3) the inadequate understanding of its members of the circumstances surrounding potential conflicts and of the conditions faced in the field by UN peacekeeping and peace enforcement operations. These weaknesses might be alleviated, but hardly cured, by having a more representative Council. Enlarging the Council by increasing geographic representation among the permanent members would almost certainly make the decision-making process more cumbersome.

Is there, then, persuasive and pressing reason for change? The answer is yes, and there is not just one reason, but several. Most fundamentally, the effectiveness of the Security Council depends very heavily on the respect in which it is held by member states. UN membership entails a weighty commitment, one that lends to the

Security Council a degree of supranational control. Members agree under the Charter that in maintaining international peace and security, the Security Council "acts in their behalf" and that they will "accept and carry out" its decisions.[5] If the interests of the majority of member states are not more adequately represented than is now the case, it is unlikely that they will, over the long run, comply with the Council's decisions. Unless the Council is made more representative its authority will be in jeopardy.

A further compelling reason for reform is that the United Nations would gain substantially from the additional strength and resources that would be derived from the permanent membership of Japan and Germany. As permanent members their financial contribution to peacekeeping undertakings would be automatically increased. They could be more readily looked to for participation in, and support of, Security Council undertakings for which both are badly needed. Just as the Security Council needs, for maximum effectiveness, to be more representative of the greatly expanded UN membership, so, also, does it need to derive the strength inherent in the permanent participation of the strongest economic powers.

Finally, cooperation between the states of the North and South in the United Nations as a whole suffers when there is disaffection among them because the Southern states, a majority of the General Assembly, feel vulnerable to the domination of a small Northern minority in consequence of the composition of the one body in the United Nations that is authorized to take action on behalf of international security. This is increasingly the situation as more and more Council actions entail involvement in internal conflicts that tend to be within the smaller states that constitute the majority of UN members.

It is only necessary to glance over the responses from member states to the Secretary-General's request for suggestions on equitable representation[6] to realize how extremely difficult it will be to reach agreement on enlarging the Council. It may prove impossible. That is why it is worth giving some thought to other, possibly supplementary, ways in which decline in respect for the Council's authority can be arrested. Enhancement of the role of the General Assembly, where all members are represented, in response to the enlarged dimensions of international security is one possibility. Restriction of the veto right of the permanent members and modification in the voting rules in the Council are among other possibilities discussed in greater detail in later chapters.

NOTES

1. When arguing the case for the veto power of the permanent members at San Francisco, the three powers insisted that it marked an improvement over the League since it meant a reduction in the number of members having the right of veto. In NATO and the Organization for Security and Cooperation in Europe (OSCE) decision making is also by consensus. This caused unfortunate delays in the availability of NATO forces for use in dealing with the conflict in the former Yugoslavia and was a major factor in the absence of effective OSCE action in this crisis.
2. Edward R. Stettinius, Jr., *Report to the President on the Results of the San Francisco Conference,* Department of State, 26 June, 1945.
3. Article 44 reads: When the Security Council has decided to use force it shall, before calling upon a member not represented on it to provide armed forces in fulfillment of the obligations assumed under Article 43, invite that member, if the member so desires, to participate in the decisions of the Security Council concerning the employment of contingents of that member's armed forces.
4. Independent Working Group on the Future of the United Nations, *The United Nations in Its Second Half-Century* (New York: Ford Foundation, 1995).
5. United Nations Charter, Articles 24 and 25.
6. Contained in UN document A/48/264, 20 July 1993.

2

TEN BALANCES FOR WEIGHING UN REFORM PROPOSALS

BRUCE RUSSETT

This is a time, following its fiftieth anniversary, for renewed interest in reforming, restructuring, and reinvigorating the United Nations. By some reasonable standards parts of the UN have worked well much of the time, and others have not. The challenges facing the organization have changed, with new emphasis on civil conflict (within rather than between states),[1] population growth, massive voluntary and involuntary migrations, environmental degradation, economic justice, expanded concepts of human rights, and belief in the possibility and the necessity of representative government. The resources the UN commands, and the will of its member states to employ the organization, are inadequate to meet those challenges.

Consequently, several major comprehensive proposals to restructure the UN have been put forth,[2] as well as many partial ones addressed to particular parts like the Security Council. Even at its creation, the UN was, for all the "realism" attached to its new institutions of collective security, also in substantial degree a "liberal internationalist" project in the sense derived from the vision of Immanuel Kant's essay *Zum Ewigen Frieden* (On Perpetual Peace). It was a holistic vision, both moral and based on experience, and not *merely* rooted in state or group self-interest.

That vision, for which we in 1995 marked the two-hundredth anniversary, saw peace as built on a solid tripod of free political institutions, networks of economic interdependence, and international law and institutions.[3] The vision was reflected, for example, in the Bretton Woods financial institutions, the United Nations Development Programme, the Commission on Human Rights and the Center for Human Rights, and the International Court of Justice.

The vision was also, in current terms, one of "human security";[4] that is, the security of states, and of their peoples, from mortal danger, a vision attentive to a broad range of human rights: political, social, and economic. In this vision, the element of international law and organization is quintessentially represented by the United Nations. The matter of direct support of a regime for peace and security from violence often focuses primarily on the Security Council, as the preeminent organ dedicated to that purpose. Yet the whole UN can do much more than that; it can indirectly undergird peace by promoting and helping to manage economic interdependence, and by supporting and protecting the political rights of representative government. In sympathy with, if not full acceptance of, this vision, therefore, it is appropriate to judge reform proposals with these Kantian or liberal internationalist criteria in mind, for they inform the contemporary discourse on the United Nations even more than they did at the Organization's founding. These criteria are subversive of authoritarian and autarchic definitions of state sovereignty, supportive of popular sovereignty in control of interdependent states. They therefore provide the basis for strengthening and actively promoting the production of representative governments in the global system. Sovereign liberal nation-states would serve as components of liberal global institutions that would have enough teeth to defend themselves against illiberal challengers.

To evaluate proposals, one must decide how well they should, and do, strike various *balances*. (Or, perhaps, how well any proposal synthesizes various opposites, or Hegelian dialectics.) Some degree of balance is needed not merely because everyone will bring different values and perspectives to the task, but because of the complexity of the social phenomena at issue. Rarely can any balance be successfully tipped all the way in one direction. In the spirit of stimulating discussion, I propose ten balances for consideration. (The number ten is fortuitous rather than intentional. However, any effort to design global institutions is a bit like playing God, so perhaps the number is not totally coincidental.) Sometimes I will illustrate the effort to strike a balance with reference to the report I know best, namely that of the Independent Working Group on the Future of the United Nations.[5] But in doing so I do not intend to offer a full explication, let alone defense, of the particular balances achieved in that Report. Some of the applications are particularly relevant to discussions about the Security Council; others are not. In general, the purpose is rather to offer a set of criteria for evaluation, leaving it to every reader to make her own or his own judgment on where a balance should be struck, and where it was struck in any individual proposal. These balances are interrelated, often closely; none operates alone.

1. The Balance between the Interests and Perspectives of States and of Broad-Based Nongovernmental Organizations (NGOs) and Other Nonstate Actors

While typically multinational in execution, the writing of such reports is unavoidably an elite enterprise. The majority of participants usually come from public sector backgrounds (e.g., service in elective, appointive, or administrative office), and therefore usually give large consideration to the interests of the state. Even those whose personal backgrounds are predominantly from civil society or NGOs are usually highly privileged members of their societies. Nonetheless, they must try and at least partially succeed in transcending their elite and statist perspectives, reflecting wider and somewhat less "top-down" views. This is not just for the sake of wider appreciation in the subsequent public dialogue, but because state elites simply do not have all the answers. While speaking the realities of power, the participants must also speak a wider version of truth to power.

2. The Balance between the Preservation and the Erosion of State Sovereignty

Ever since the Treaty of Westphalia, state juridical sovereignty has been the fundamental legal and ideological principle (and also myth) undergirding the world system. The United Nations is an organization comprising sovereign states; it is neither a world government nor an assembly of peoples. Elites understandably want to retain the sovereignty of the states they control, as do most of their citizens. No reform proposal that fails to preserve, and in some ways even to strengthen, state sovereignty can hope for a favorable reception from those who have the power to enact the proposal. The reform must be acceptable to the vast majority of governments, as consistent with their sovereignty.

Yet, at the same time, states' practical sovereignty has in many areas been eroded in the modern world.[6] Some of these erosions have happened consciously and voluntarily—most strikingly in the case of the European Union, in other instances by a variety of treaty commitments binding states to common legal norms and procedures. Some others have been intended but involuntary, as when extreme repression or humanitarian distress becomes the basis for international intervention in what would normally be the domestic affairs of a state (e.g., Iraq, Haiti). Still others have been both involuntary and unintended, as when states lose to international banks and currency speculators much of their ability to control their national budgets and foreign exchange rates, or their ability to manage the effect of transnational flows of pollution or the erosion of resources in the global commons. Humanitarian disasters and massive refugee flows from civil conflict may defy the practical ability of a state to insulate itself and its policies from events in its neighbors. Indeed, the collapse of civil authority in a country (e.g., Somalia) may mean that there is no government capable of exercising the practical rights of sovereignty to which the country may still nominally be entitled.

In these and other instances the role of an international organization may well come down to that of helping to strengthen or even rebuild civil authority, and hence enabling the government to exercise certain of its sovereign rights (to manage its economy, to limit the effects of pollution, to restore a system of public order and justice) that it could not otherwise exert. International organizations must therefore strike some balance between replacing and building the sovereignty of their member states. This is true even when the proponents of a particular reform consciously wish to diminish state sovereignty in certain areas. No other course will be acceptable.

The delicate nature of this balance is illustrated by the problem of providing assistance to "collapsed states," or, as the task is called more tactfully in the Report of the Independent Working Group (p. 53), the "coordination of efforts to rebuild weakened societies under stress." In such cases the UN or other legally sanctioned external actor must try to rebuild the state's administrative, political, judicial, and economic structure so that it can again exercise its legal sovereign rights—but in a form that respects human rights broadly, and that involves some supervision based both on an international consensus and some agreement between the international organization and those local authorities that do function. It implies some mixture of at least temporary voluntary and involuntary surrender of formal sovereignty, for the sake of regaining essential elements of real sovereignty later.[7]

The mechanism proposed by the Independent Working Group for coordinating the rebuilding of a "state under stress" is a new Social Council, working in collaboration with a new Economic Council. (Both would be new principal organs of the UN, replacing ECOSOC; the membership of each would be chosen with regard to accepted international principles of representation.) But the Social Council would be empowered to act only "with the consent of the local government if it retains authority," (p. 38) or, if not, as authorized by the Security Council and some political groups within the country concerned. Obviously this is a very difficult balance: the UN must not be seen as a neocolonial usurper of state sovereignty, but as ultimately restoring it. And if weak states are to permit it to assume certain "conservancy" functions, it must have at its disposal—from the international community—the very substantial human and material resources needed truly to restore effective and humane government.

3. The Balance between Practicality and Vision

Here the balance is between what should be done, and what can be done. What will states more or less readily accept, and what can they successfully be persuaded to accept, by other states or by their own constituents and civil society? How much should they be subjected to higher aspirations even if those aspirations are not readily or plausibly achievable in the midterm future? Visionaries are by definition impractical, yet some of both qualities are necessary to make any reform worth pursuing.

A relevant illustration here is the Independent Working Group's treatment of financing the UN. The Report makes all the right more-or-less practical noises about the need for greater efficiency in the UN's use of existing resources, the need for states to pay their legally mandated assessments in full and on time, and the need for revision of the assessment formula to mitigate existing perceived inequities. Yet it admits that the requirements of enforcement, peacebuilding, development, human rights, preservation of the commons, and so forth are likely vastly to exceed what member states will be willing to pay as assessments.

Thus the Report also creatively calls (p. 48) for "additional sources of funding that are not dependent on the political and budgetary constraints under which most governments operate," to take the form of "some sort of levy on the utilization of the global commons." It recognizes that it will be very hard to decide what form that tax might take.[8] Any global tax will face both enormous political resistance from those on whom it is levied and enormous problems of administrative difficulty. In the current environment of domestic politics in many countries, instituting any form of tax seems unthinkable.

It is not just a matter of cost. A reasonable case can be made for tight fiscal control over any organization. The need always for the UN to persuade member governments to pay their dues provides a powerful restraint on the UN; imposition of some type of global tax could dissolve states' existing fiscal control over the UN. In proposing such a tax, therefore, the Working Group puts an important and even necessary idea on the agenda for discussion, but also pushes the envelope of practicality. Serious attention to maintaining some adequate power of the purse on behalf of those who in one way or another will pay most of the bills is essential. A solution, possibly keyed to functions of the proposed Economic Council, need not be beyond reach.

4. The Balance between Power (or Effectiveness) and Legitimacy (or Justice)

This balance is closely related to the previous one. Nothing can happen without the capability or power to do it, and the willingness to exert that power. In the global arena, major UN activities must have the approval, and usually the active participation and support, of the most powerful states in the system. Although the World Bank and the International Monetary Fund owe their existence to the needs of economic justice, they cannot violate the wishes of the states that provide their principal funding. The Security Council cannot, given the veto, embark on an operation against the wishes of a permanent member. Nor should it do so without assurances of financial and military commitment from the major powers whose active participation in some form will be necessary. Power talks, and acts. No action in the absence of adequate power will be effective. And power will not act in a particular case unless each major state in the United Nations deems the action to be worthwhile by its definition (broad or narrow, immediate or long term) of its national interest.

If it is also to be effective, neither the UN in general, nor the Security Council in particular, will ever be very "democratic" if democracy is defined either as one-state one-vote or, over the whole world, one-person one-vote. It is no coincidence that the Security Council, with the potential and some history of exerting strong powers of enforcement under Chapter VII, is probably the least democratic UN organ. The Security Council can, when its members so choose, make or break states. The powerful states represented on the Council, and who would be principally tasked with carrying out enforcement action, are unwilling to be committed by a vote that does not reflect their economic and military differential. By contrast, the General Assembly, often derided as a talk shop and certainly with no formal power of enforcement, is one of the most democratic (one-state one-vote) organs.

Democracy within a country can succeed only where there are serious limitations on the exercise of coercive violence and limitations on the concentration of economic power (income and wealth). Additionally, democratic government requires some community of basic values among the populace, or at least some protection for the rights and values of minorities. The international system, however, lacks all these conditions. Military power for state violence is concentrated overwhelmingly in the hands of the five permanent members (nuclear weapons) or a single superpower with global reach (nearly half of all world military expenditures). The 20 percent of the world's population living in the wealthiest countries receives 85 percent of global income—a concentration far higher than within any single country, rich or poor. Despite some convergence on values, one cannot yet talk fully persuasively about a community of basic values in the world. Under such circumstances, and however one laments it, the rich and powerful will not surrender real power to any organization controlled by a majority of states or individuals. One can perhaps hope for greater consultation and transparency, greater deference to the needs of those not rich and powerful, and some opening of the system to the influence of nongovernmental organizations. But democratization of the UN in the form of majority rule is a pipe dream. (Pipe dreams have their origin in opium, not tobacco.) It could happen, if at all, only in a UN deprived of the capacity to accomplish anything.

On the other hand, power cannot long be exercised in raw form, divorced from concepts of equity and legitimacy. Despite all the Security Council's necessity to represent power, and to maintain the procedures and small size required for timely and judicious action, its legitimacy will be questioned to the degree it is seen as no more than a concert of great powers—especially of rich industrial ones. The Council's recent greater readiness to invoke economic sanctions against member states enhances this perception. The greater the authority of the Security Council, with its Northern dominance, the greater the domination of the entire UN by the North. (The International Court of Justice, like the General Assembly, is more South-dominated, but even so it refuses to challenge the authority of the Council to take actions.)

If the Security Council adds Germany and Japan as permanent members without also adding some major less-developed countries it risks losing legitimacy in the eyes of the great majority of UN member states. In turn, however, the more numerous and diverse the permanent members wielding veto power, the more difficult it will become to act promptly and effectively when the world community wants action. E. H. Carr caught the problem of the Council of the League of Nations: "Increases in membership . . . gave a permanent preponderance to the minor Powers. The Council, in becoming more 'representative,' lost much of its effectiveness as a political instrument."[9] An ineffective Security Council will not retain legitimacy either. Hence the incentive, when adding any veto-wielding members, to restrict the scope of the veto, such as to the realm of military action that might threaten a great power's vital interest—as wished by most of the UN's American and British founders.[10]

Advocacy of Security Council reform carries the explicit or implicit perspective that states left outside the formal structure carry the potential to disrupt the system, and therefore they need to be brought inside. Yet the impetus to reform is weakened by the absence of players on the outside with the ability and willingness, at present, actually to disrupt it seriously. Developing countries are not yet powerful enough as individuals, or united enough as a collectivity, to do so. In principle Germany and Japan might be able to do so, but to threaten such action, even implicitly, would completely undermine their argument that they are now fully responsible world citizens. They can put forth the normative argument why their states ought justly to be represented, but in arguing from a position of power they must limit themselves to the case for what their power might contribute to collective goals, and not to any ability to pursue private goals.

So long as arguments about disruptive power cannot be made, and the implicit danger is not regarded as serious, the impetus to reform is weak. Admitting new centers of power to the formal structure risks a loss of ability to make prompt and appropriate decisions for the organization, and a loss of power by those who currently hold it in the Council, against the still small threat of disruption. Current power wielders, and many states currently satisfied with Council decisions if not themselves powerful, would prefer a relatively weak Council they can control to a stronger one over whose decisions they would have less power. Furthermore, the Security Council has already experienced substantial change in its informal procedures, providing, for example, for serious consultation with Germany and Japan on collective security actions. (It is hardly imaginable that an expensive operation would be undertaken without tacit German and Japanese consent.) Thus the need to change formal structures and voting rights may not be immediate. Much of whatever restructuring does happen will be symbolic, directed in large part to satisfying domestic constituencies that their states are in fact regarded internationally as legitimate actors.

The balance of power between the Security Council (dominated by the great powers) and the General Assembly (a relatively weak organ in which the NAM is predominant) also needs continuing scrutiny. The Council is, and will remain, charged with the responsibility to make decisions to engage in enforcement actions under Chapter VII. Nevertheless, because of post–Cold War assertions of the Council's authority—as in actions against Iraq and Libya—the balance has shifted more toward the Council and away from the Assembly than was true a decade or two ago. One measure at least to involve the Assembly in an advisory role might be to establish a "Consultation Committee" broadly representative of the General Assembly's membership. Whenever the Security Council planned to take action under Chapter VII it would be expected to inform the Committee, and to solicit its views throughout the crisis. This in no way implies a veto for the Committee, but the requirement would amount "to more than mere notification."[11]

5. The Balance between Particularity and Universality

This is the dilemma between, on the one hand, respect for national and subnational cultural values, including different priorities and conceptions of human rights, and, on the other hand, the proclamation and widespread acceptance of the principle that there *are* universal human rights and substantial (if often vague, contested, and incomplete) agreement as to the nature of those rights. The Universal Declaration of Human Rights and its subsequent conventions, protocols, and agreements have been widely ratified, and embodied in the documents emanating from major UN Conferences. Despite the protests of Asian authoritarians, religious fundamentalists, and rich country postmodernists, there *is* a real degree of consensus.

Nonetheless, the need to respect cultural and political diversity, to balance individual rights with conceptions of group rights, within states as well as between them, lies at the core of intrastate and interstate peace. Devising principles, procedures, and institutions to do so requires a never-ending and ever-contestable balancing act. States need some protection from the threat of disintegration. But minority rights need protection from the potential tyranny of the majority—even sometimes from a democratically chosen majority. For any proposed increment in the powers and purposes of international institutions, this balance is crucially related to the sovereignty balance.

6. The Balance between Civil and Political Rights on One End and Economic Rights on the Other

This balance is closely related to the preceding one. It is widely claimed that, especially for poor countries, satisfaction of economic rights (basic material needs) must come first; that civil and political rights are "luxury" goods to be obtained only later—if ever. This view was common in Marxist regimes, and remains powerful in rapidly developing capitalist systems operating in "strong states." Of course there must be some room for the determination and application of priorities; all good things do not go together in lockstep. Most rich countries are democratically governed and many poor ones are ruled by authoritarian regimes. Yet there are numerous exceptions in both groups. Qatar, Singapore, and the United Arab Emirates have higher per capita incomes than do Canada and France. India has experienced decades of substantially democratic rule while ranking among the lowest income countries, as have other states. But systematic empirical evidence of the *necessity* of sharp trade-offs of economic against political and civil rights simply does not exist. The notion that political opposition must be repressed in the interest of development is, as a generalization, a lie. An excellent review of the scientific literature on political and economic development summarizes the situation well:

> There is no evidence that, on average, a democracy with civil liberties is costly in terms of economic development. If anything it may be the other way around, that a democracy with civil liberties promotes economic development. . . . But establishing democratic institutions is not the "deus ex machina" that resolves all the problems of development. A sound and stable political-economic development is essential.[12]

Representative government can facilitate balanced and equitable economic development in the following ways: An equitable distribution of income, and political stability, are important contributors to successful growth.[13] By providing stable, legitimate governance and a restrained rule of law, representative government strengthens the property rights necessary to encourage long-term investment.[14] By providing a base of widespread access to the political system, it discourages the engorgement of inefficient state monopolies and prevents secret environmental abuses of the kind that have emerged from the communist era in Eastern Europe and the former Soviet Union. It offers some check on corruption by officials who would otherwise operate behind opaque barriers of state security and without any inquiry by free public media. (Zairean president Mobutu Sese Seko exemplifies the kleptocracy of a leadership whose interest in economic development extends only to enriching itself.) Mass famines occur *only* in political systems where information can be suppressed and protest repressed.[15]

In particular instances there will always be an element of contradiction between some kinds of rights and others. But they are not inevitably in any kind of severe dialectic. The elements of complementarity on the whole outweigh those of contradiction. Those times when they do come into conflict, and are not sufficiently mutually reinforcing, may be precisely the times for international organizations to use their influence to preserve a balance, for example by standing up for the principles of representative government as well as the necessity for achieving decent material living conditions.

7. The Balance between Enforcement and Neutrality

The idea of an international organization empowered to *enforce* the protection of basic human rights rightly causes fear, not only among those judged guilty in a particular instance but among weak states everywhere. But it also represents the hope of many vulnerable individuals and oppressed peoples. This tension cannot be avoided in any discussion of human rights, and is of course integrally related to the sovereignty balance. In traditional peacekeeping operations—in which the UN forces were on the ground with the consent of the parties, were authorized to shoot only in self-defense, and were not supposed to take sides or otherwise become a party to the conflict—the balance was overwhelmingly on the side of neutrality. Yet sometimes "neutrality" effectively would mean taking the side of the strong against the weak, without regard to judgments about justice. The UN has also operated (more rarely to be sure, but with Korea and Iraq the prime exhibits) as an agent of collective security, coercing a named aggressor and trying to enforce a settlement that manifestly favored one side.

"Peace enforcement," as it emerged in Boutros Boutros-Ghali's *An Agenda for Peace,* represents a precarious effort to balance enforcement and impartiality, using force as "a provisional measure" when deemed necessary to avert large-scale humanitarian disaster.[16] The need arises in the context of increasingly common civil wars and breakdowns of order, and requires an immensely difficult balancing act. Somalia, Rwanda, and Bosnia all illustrate, in different ways, the hazards. Perhaps most of the time the UN will lack the consensus, the will, and even the capability to engage in peace enforcement. Writing—and if necessary adjusting—the mandate for every such activity offers a formidable challenge. But sometimes the international community, acting through its designated institutions, will decide it to be necessary. The Independent Working Group, for example, calls for establishing a small UN Rapid Reaction Force, available for urgent deployment by the Security Council so as to prevent certain dangerous political conditions from deteriorating into chaos and disaster. The Force would be capable not only of a peacekeeping mission, but (limited however by its size), able to "provide security for UN personnel; hold an airport . . . ; establish one or more safe areas for the civilian population; limit escalation and assist in ending the violence. . . ." These are in large degree peace enforcement tasks, not those of traditional peacekeeping. They are also distinct from collective security enforcement by heavily armed units, which the UN dare undertake only when its key members are confident they are prepared to stay the course.

8. The Balance between Specificity and Plasticity of the Charter

The UN Charter has proven to be a reasonably flexible instrument. For instance, it has been possible to stretch the Charter, for purposes of maintaining "international peace and security," to modify in de facto fashion the Article 2(7) prohibition of intervention "in matters which are essentially within the domestic jurisdiction of any state,"[17] and to invent the institution of peacekeeping despite the absence of any explicit Charter authorization for it. Nevertheless, it is extremely difficult to amend the Charter formally since amendments require approval by two-thirds of the General Assembly and then ratification by two-thirds of the member states, including approval by all five of the permanent members of the Security Council. Over its 50-year history, the only amendments to make it through that process have been for one enlargement of the nonpermanent membership of the Security Council and two stages of enlargement of ECOSOC. The problem remains how to write—or now, when and how as necessary to modify—a foundational document that will preserve the foundation while underpinning a structure that can expand, contract, and change its form and function in response to new and unforeseen power realities and challenges.

9. The Balance between Uniformity and Diversity of Purpose

A common criticism of the UN has been of the uncoordinated nature of its various units and specialized agencies. Indeed, they not infrequently pursue conflicting goals, whether as part of a peacebuilding effort in El Salvador or in delivering humanitarian relief in Africa.[18] At best the result is the waste of very limited resources; at worst it is outright failure. It seems intolerable to have different organs working at bureaucratic cross-purposes.

Yet some diversity of goal and doctrine has its value. In the arena of economic development, the UN—and the members of the economic profession who advise or comment on its policies—has yet to come up with a coherent, unified theory of economic development. It is not much more attractive to imagine all economic development assistance to be administered on the model of the World Bank than on the model of UNDP. Nor can we ever expect to see complete agreement on concept or practice between the rich states from which development funds must come and the poor ones which constitute the locus and object of development projects. The Independent Working Group's proposal for a new Economic Council contains a built-in and unavoidable tension. It would be charged (p. 52) "to integrate the work of all UN agencies and international institutions, programs and offices engaged in economic issues . . . promote the harmonization of the fiscal, monetary and trade policies of member states and encourage international cooperation on issues of technology and resources, indebtedness, and the functioning of commodity markets." Yet it also encourages different development approaches. Some increased integration and harmonization is surely desirable. Very much is surely not desirable nor, in a world of sovereign states, possible. How and where the balance will be struck lies in the realm of a continuing political process that will always also reflect the competing claims of the balance of effectiveness and legitimacy (justice).

10. The Balance of Interests

Governance of and by the UN is, like all instances of governance, a political process in which numerous interests exert claims and can resist claims. The UN's constitutional structure guarantees a plethora of actors with de facto if not de jure veto power. Hence any reform proposal will have to have something to please most everyone, as well as, in the best satirical tradition, something to offend most everyone. The trick is to get the balance right, not just in any single reform proposal (expand the Security Council, create a new Economic Council and a new Social Council, institute some new mode of financing the organization), but in a package of proposals. No single reform recommendation, whether for the Security Council or another organ, can be considered in isolation. Nor will any large acceptable package be put together without long negotiation and intense public debate, in UN halls and around the world. The task of reforming and renewing the United Nations is at heart a political task, as arduous as it is essential.

NOTES

1. Donald C. F. Daniel and Brad C. Hayes, eds., *Beyond Traditional Peacekeeping* (New York: St. Martin's, 1995); Lori Fisler Damrosch, ed., *Enforcing Restraint: Collective Intervention in Internal Conflicts* (New York: Council on Foreign Relations, 1993).
2. Major ones include Erskine Childers with Brian Urquhart, *Renewing the United Nations System* (Uppsala, Sweden: Dag Hammarskjold Foundation, 1994); South Commission, *Reforming the United Nations: A View from the South* (Geneva: South Centre, 1995); Commission on Global Governance, *Our Global Neighborhood* (New York: Oxford University Press, 1995); Independent Working Group on the Future of the United Nations, *The United Nations in Its Second Half-Century* (New York: Ford Foundation, 1995).
3. Bruce Russett, *Grasping the Democratic Peace: Principles for a Post - Cold War World* (Princeton, N.J.: Princeton University Press, 1993); John Oneal, Frances Oneal, Zeev Maoz, and Bruce Russett, "The Liberal Peace: Interdependence, Democracy, and International Conflict, 1950 - 1985," *Journal of Peace Research* 33 (1996), pp. 11-28.
4. This term is used explicitly by the Commission on Global Governance and the Independent Working Group (see en. 2); see also United Nations Development Programme, *Human Development Report,* 1994 (New York: Oxford University Press, 1994).
5. I served, with Paul Kennedy, as Co-Director of the Secretariat of the Working Group. For that reason I avoid commenting at all on the particulars of other reports. A Kantian vision certainly underlay my contributions, and whereas I believe Professor Kennedy and most—perhaps all—of the members of the Working Group implicitly shared that vision in some degree, neither they nor the Ford Foundation, which funded the effort, are responsible for any of the remarks in this chapter. Nor would I pretend that all of the balances proposed here were ever considered overtly or consciously; they are, however, relevant both to post hoc evaluation and to any effort to synthesize recommendations from the various studies and reports.
6. See Hedley Bull and Adam Watson, eds., *The Evolution of International Society: A Comparative Historical Analysis* (London: Routledge, 1994); Mark Zacher, "The Decaying Pillars of the Westphalian System," in Ernst-Otto Czempiel and James Rosenau, eds., *Governance without Government: Order and Change in World Politics* (Cambridge: Cambridge University Press, 1992); D. J. Elkins, *Beyond Sovereignty: Territory and Political Economy in the Twenty-First Century* (Toronto: University of Toronto Press, 1995); Michael Barnett, "The New UN Politics of Peace," *Global Governance* 1 (1995), pp. 79-98.
7. Steven Ratner, *The New UN Peacekeeping: Building Peace in Lands of Conflict after the Cold War* (New York: St. Martin's, 1995); I. William Zartman, ed., *Collapsed States: The Disintegration and Restoration of Legitimate Authority* (Boulder, Col.: Lynne Rienner, 1995).

8. For some possibilities, see the special issue, "The UN at Fifty: Policy and Financing Alternatives," *Futures: The Journal of Forecasting, Planning, and Policy* 27 (1995); Dragoljub Najman and Hans d'Orville, *Towards a New Multilateralism: Funding Global Priorities* (Paris and New York: Independent Commission on Population and Quality of Life, 1995); Ruben Mendez, "Paying for Peace and Development," *Foreign Policy* 100 (1995), pp. 19-32.
9. Edward Hallett Carr, *The Twenty Years' Crisis, 1919-1939* (London, Macmillan, 1942), p. 39.
10. Robert C. Hilderbrand, *Dumbarton Oaks: The Origins of the United Nations and the Search for Postwar Security* (Chapel Hill: University of North Carolina Press, 1990).
11. W. Michael Reisman, "The Constitutional Crisis in the United Nations," *American Journal of International Law* 87 (1993), p. 99.
12. Alberto Alesina and Roberto Perotti, "The Political Economy of Growth: A Critical Survey of the Recent Literature," *World Bank Economic Review* 8 (1994), pp. 354-55.
13. Alesina and Perotti, "The Political Economy of Growth," pp. 351-74; see also Ross Burkhart and Michael Lewis-Beck, "Comparative Democracy: The Economic Development Thesis," *American Political Science Review* 88 (1994), pp. 903-10; Adam Przeworski and Fernando Limongi, "Political Regimes and Economic Growth," *Journal of Economic Perspectives* 7 (1993), pp. 51-70; John F. Helliwell, "Empirical Linkages between Democracy and Economic Growth," *British Journal of Political Science* 24 (1994), pp. 175-98; Robert Putnam, *Making Democracy Work: Civic Traditions in Modern Italy* (Princeton: Princeton University Press, 1993).
14. Mancur Olson, "Dictatorship, Democracy, and Development," *American Political Science Review* 87 (1993), pp. 567-76.
15. Amartya Sen, *Poverty and Famine* (New York: Oxford University Press, 1981).
16. Boutros Boutros-Ghali, *An Agenda for Peace* (New York: United Nations, 1992), p. 26.
17. Article 39 becomes the escape clause to permit intervention: "The Security Council shall determine the existence of any threat to the peace, breach of the peace, or act of aggression and shall make recommendations, or decide what measures shall be taken . . . to restore international peace and security."
18. See Alvaro de Soto and Graciana del Castillo, "Obstacles to Peacebuilding," *Foreign Policy* 94 (1994), pp. 69-83; also Eva Bertram, "Reinventing Government: The Promise and Perils of Peacebuilding," *Journal of Conflict Resolution* 39 (1995), pp. 387-418.

3

THE NEW POLITICS OF VOTING ALIGNMENTS IN THE GENERAL ASSEMBLY

SOO YEON KIM
AND BRUCE RUSSETT

The end of the Cold War saw the dismantling of the bipolar system that had characterized international politics for more than 40 years. The ensuing changes reflect a new era in international politics, and raise questions about which issues are emerging with new importance and about how the preferences of countries are aligned on those issues. The United Nations General Assembly, as a forum in which international politics is played out, can provide insight into the content and texture of these changes. The General Assembly offers a unique context in which to study post–Cold War international politics, providing a great deal of information about the issues most salient to its member states and about their preferences. It also provides information and insights essential to an understanding of the political implications of change in the Security Council.

This chapter identifies and analyzes the patterns in member state preferences in the form of voting alignments on the issues that have figured most prominently in General Assembly debates. Our primary objective is descriptive inference; that is, to illustrate the unobserved underlying issue dimensions of General Assembly roll-call votes and the alignments inherent in these votes by analyzing General Assembly voting records. The analysis covers resolutions put to a roll-call vote in the 46th through 48th sessions (1991 through 1993). We delineate the issue dimensions that drive the activities of the General Assembly and analyze influences on the voting patterns of member states. These patterns have changed greatly since the end of the Cold War. The East-West division no longer prevails in deliberations; a North-South cleavage has superseded Cold War alignments, giving rise to state preferences defined along developmental lines.

Earlier Patterns

A study by Hayward Alker marks an early stage in a body of research that has sought to identify issue dimensions and voting alignments in the UN General Assembly since its establishment in 1945.[1] The studies as a group span the entire history of the United Nations and, through applications of different statistical techniques, largely confirm one another's findings, especially in the delineation of voting blocs. The literature is thus consistent in its substantive results across different methods, inspiring confidence in studies that illustrate the evolution of state behavior in the United Nations.

Alker found two major *behavioral* voting alignments, East-West and North-South, in the 16th General Assembly (1961). In an alternative interpretation, which lays the basis for our presentation here, he identified four main *substantive* issue dimensions underlying roll-call votes, which he labeled self-determination, Cold War and related membership questions, UN supranationalism, and Muslim questions.[2] Together these four issues accounted for 85 percent of the variance in General Assembly roll-call votes.

An expanded study of four different General Assembly sessions—1947, 1952, 1957, and 1961—by Alker and Russett found three of these substantive issue dimensions—Cold War, colonialism, and supranationalism—to occur repeatedly.[3] The Cold War dimension separated the voting groups into Communists versus the "West." The colonial dimension divided the colonial powers from the former colonies. Finally, supranationalism distinguished those that favored a stronger United Nations from those that did not. These three issue dimensions, or "super-issues," accounted for more than half of the variance in roll-call voting in each of the four General Assembly sessions. Two other super-issues, albeit with less explanatory power, included intervention in southern Africa and matters concerning Palestine. These five factors together regularly accounted for 59 to 70 percent of all the variance in roll-call voting in each session. A study of the 18th session by Russett identified the same five factors, which accounted for two-thirds of the total variance and of which the Cold War issue was most prominent. He also identified voting groups. For the 18th session, he found five major voting blocs, in addition to two small groups and several marginal countries, and suggested that a simplified East-West-Neutral categorization could be misleading. In another study, Russett found four major voting blocs in 1952, and four major and four smaller groups in 1957.[4] Later studies of General Assembly voting behavior generally confirmed these findings.[5]

More recently, Steven Holloway analyzed five General Assembly sessions—1946, 1955, 1965,1975, and 1985.[6] He found that, by 1985, three large voting blocs had formed. The most cohesive was the Warsaw Pact group, which also included a small group of radical Third World states including Cuba, Afghanistan, Vietnam, and Syria. The second large voting group was the Non-Aligned Movement (NAM) bloc, which appeared to have retained its cohesion through 1985, ostensibly through the organizational efforts of the NAM and Group of 77. The third bloc, consisting of Western or Organization for Economic Cooperation and Development (OECD) countries, was located far from the first two groups and spread over a large space, reflecting the wide spectrum of left-to-right differences among its members. Holloway found these groups to be stable over time, especially between 1975 and 1985. In 1985 Poland appeared as a point separate from the Soviet Union for the first time, reflecting the pre-glasnost configuration presaging the loosening of the Soviet bloc.

Previous studies of General Assembly voting records have thus focused on voting alignments, which delineate the major voting groups to be found among member states, and issue dimensions, which characterize the clusters of resolutions put to a roll-call vote that in turn give rise to distinct voting alignments. The most useful studies identify voting alignments on particular issues or issue dimensions. Since voting alignments do vary greatly over different issue dimensions, studies that identify voting alignments regardless of the issues that give rise to them often obscure important information. Thus we shall follow a procedure that preserves the two kinds of information, first identifying the major issue dimensions and then showing the voting alignments on each dimension.

Data, Measurement, and Methods

Our primary data are derived from voting records on those resolutions put to a roll-call vote in the 46th through 48th sessions of the United Nations General Assembly, spanning the sessions beginning in each of the years 1991-93. Virtually all the resolutions that come up for a vote in the General Assembly pass; in the period analyzed here almost 80 percent of the total of 957 votes conducted were unanimous. Another 71 votes were so nearly unanimous as to convey little additional information on states' alignments, so we excluded them. Our analysis examines the votes of 150 countries on the other 131 votes on which a formal roll call was taken. We ranked the votes so as to reflect as closely as possible the distribution of voting preferences for the particular resolution. They are then standardized so as to assign a zero—the truly middle position—to those countries that were absent or not participating at the time of these roll-call votes.[7] Since it would be difficult to justify the assignment of a neutral position to countries that are absent from a large fraction of the roll-call votes, we exclude countries that were absent or not participating for more than 30 percent of the total number of votes.

Factor analysis reduces a set of variables, based on their correlations, to a smaller number of variables, known as "factors," that are the theoretical constructs that are latent to the variables and of which the variables are indicators. This technique is thus appropriate for determining which resolutions produce similar voting patterns and how many groupings of such similarities can account for countries' patterns of roll-call votes. With the variables reduced to their underlying dimensions, it then becomes possible to offer an interpretation of what these issue dimensions are and to identify the major voting groups with respect to them. Furthermore, since the voting patterns are delineated separately for each issue dimension, it is also possible to illustrate the degree of consistency of countries' voting alignments across dimensions.

We will concentrate on the rotated solution when discussing the voting alignments and the issue dimensions. The unrotated solution identifies the factors that capture, sequentially, the most variance in roll-call votes. By contrast, the rotated solution maximizes the loadings, or correlations, of the resolutions across several factors, not just the first. These results typically show which substantive clusters of resolutions contribute most to the voting alignments.

Findings: Issues and Alignments

We identify, in order: the major sets of substantive issues on which states divide in the General Assembly, the positions various states occupy on these issues, and the degree to which regionally or politically defined states cluster together in similar positions. Three major factors in the rotated solution account for approximately 68 percent of the variance in the roll-call votes.[8] That is, three major issue dimensions, or super-issues, account for most of the variation in voting patterns in the three General Assembly sessions. Resolutions that share similar voting patterns are relatively evenly distributed among the three sessions. Tables 3.1a, 3.1b, and 3.1c present the list of resolutions with factor loadings of 0.50 or greater on each issue dimension in the rotated solution.

The first factor accounts for just over half (50.5 percent) of all the variance in voting. It is produced by resolutions addressing a wide spectrum of separate subissues. The diversity of subissues in itself distinguishes these findings from earlier studies of General Assembly voting patterns, which readily identified the most prevalent issue dimension to be an East-West one defined principally by Cold War issues. The end of the Cold War removed the East-West ideological and geopolitical issues from the UN's agenda, and left as dominant a wide range of issues addressing economic inequities and development; self-determination of colonies and former colonies, of which a major subset concerned South Africa and Palestine; and great-power military capabilities. Many of these issues form part of the recently emerged global agenda of "human security," which concerns development, human rights, and international security defined broadly. But notably omitted from this list of issues is attention to political rights other than in the context of colonial or postcolonial rule (see Table 3.1b).

Interpretation of the inductively derived factors is inevitably somewhat subjective, but perhaps the best, if imperfect, single descriptive label for this array of issues is "self-determination," or, more inclusively, "self-determination and disarmament." Self-determination reflects the South's concern with neocolonialism as well as classic colonialism. Despite its sometime support of national

TABLE 3.1A
Roll-Call Votes Correlated with "Self-Determination and Disarmament"
VARIANCE EXPLAINED: 50.5%

FACTOR LOADING		RESOLUTION
COLONIALISM		
0.91	46/117	HUMAN RIGHTS AND FUNDAMENTAL FREEDOMS
0.91	48/101	UN AFRICAN INSTITUTE
0.91	48/46	INDEPENDENCE TO COLONIAL COUNTRIES
0.91	48/421	ACTIVITIES ARRANGEMENTS BY COLONIAL POWERS
0.91	47/89	UN AFRICAN INSTITUTE
0.91	48/123	HUMAN RIGHTS AND FUNDAMENTAL FREEDOMS
0.90	46/89	SELF-D HUMAN RIGHTS—USE OF MERCENARIES
0.90	47/84	SELF-D HUMAN RIGHTS—USE OF MERCENARIES
0.90	46/153	UN AFRICAN INSTITUTE
0.90	46/210	COERCION OF DEVELOPING COUNTRIES
0.90	48/92	SELF-D HUMAN RIGHTS—USE OF MERCENARIES
0.89	46/84	INTERNATIONAL CONVENTION ON APARTHEID
0.88	47/29	OBSERVER STATUS NATL LIBERATION MOVEMENTS
0.88	47/81	INTERNATIONAL CONVENTION ON APARTHEID
0.88	46/65	INDEPENDENCE TO COLONIAL COUNTRIES
0.87	48/168	COERCION OF DEVELOPING COUNTRIES
0.87	48/47	INDEPENDENCE TO COLONIAL COUNTRIES
0.87	46/64	INDEPENDENCE TO COLONIAL COUNTRIES
0.86	47/16	INDEPENDENCE TO COLONIAL COUNTRIES
0.86	48/89	INTERNATIONAL CONVENTION ON APARTHEID
0.86	47/116g	COMMISSION AGAINST APARTHEID IN SPORTS
0.85	47/15	INDEPENDENCE TO COLONIAL COUNTRIES
0.84	47/116e	COLLABORATION WITH SOUTH AFRICA
0.84	46/87	RIGHT OF PEOPLES TO SELF-DETERMINATION
0.84	47/137	HUMAN RIGHTS AND FUNDAMENTAL FREEDOMS
0.83	47/82	RIGHT OF PEOPLES TO SELF-DETERMINATION
0.82	48/94	RIGHT OF PEOPLES TO SELF-DETERMINATION
0.82	46/79c	COLLABORATION WITH SOUTH AFRICA
0.81	46/130	NATL SOVEREIGNTY AND NON-INTERFERENCE
0.80	47/130	NATL SOVEREIGNTY AND NON-INTERFERENCE
0.79	48/124	NATL SOVEREIGNTY AND NON-INTERFERENCE

TABLE 3.1A (CONT'D):
Roll-Call Votes Correlated with "Self-Determination and Disarmament"

FACTOR LOADING		RESOLUTION
COLONIALISM (CONTINUED)		
0.77	47/9	COMORIAN ISLAND OF MAYOTTE
0.77	48/15	RESTITUTION OF CULTURAL PROPERTY
0.76	46/10	RESTITUTION OF CULTURAL PROPERTY
0.76	46/9	COMORIAN ISLAND OF MAYOTTE
0.75	46/79e	OIL EMBARGO AGAINST SOUTH AFRICA
0.75	47/116d	OIL EMBARGO AGAINST SOUTH AFRICA
0.73	48/56	COMORIAN ISLAND OF MAYOTTE
0.70	48/53	DISSEMINATION OF INFO ON DECOLONIZATION
0.70	46/72	DISSEMINATION OF INFO ON DECOLONIZATION
0.69	47/24	DISSEMINATION OF INFO ON DECOLONIZATION
0.67	46/79b	SPECIAL COMMITTEE AGAINST APARTHEID
0.64	48/52	INDEPENDENCE TO COLONIAL COUNTRIES
0.62	47/23	INDEPENDENCE TO COLONIAL COUNTRIES
0.62	46/71	INDEPENDENCE TO COLONIAL COUNTRIES
INTERNATIONAL SECURITY—GENERAL		
0.94	48/76	CONCLUDING DOC 12TH SPECIAL UNGA SESSION
0.94	48/83	DECLARATION STRENGTHENING OF INTL SECURITY
0.92	46/49	INDIAN OCEAN AS ZONE OF PEACE
0.92	47/53c	CONVENTION PROHIBITING USE OF NUCLEAR WEAPONS
0.92	47/59	INDIAN OCEAN AS ZONE OF PEACE
0.92	46/37c	NUCLEAR ARMS FREEZE
0.91	46/37d	UN REGIONAL CENTERS PEACE DISARMAMENT
0.91	46/38b	COMPREHENSIVE PROGRAM DISARMAMENT
0.91	47/60a	DECLARATION STRENGTHENING OF INTL SECURITY
0.91	47/53e	NUCLEAR ARMS FREEZE
0.90	46/52	DEVELOPMENT OF INTERNATIONAL LAW FOR NIEO
0.89	46/38c	REPORT CONFERENCE ON DISARMAMENT
0.88	46/28	AMENDMT TREATY BANNING NUCLEAR TESTS
0.88	47/43	SCI & TECH DEVELOPMENT AND INTL SECURITY
0.88	48/69	AMENDMENT TREATY BANNING NUCLEAR TESTS
0.88	48/82	INDIAN OCEAN AS ZONE OF PEACE
0.87	48/66	SCI & TECH DEVELOPMENT AND INTL SECURITY

TABLE 3.1A (CONT'D):
Roll-Call Votes Correlated with "Self-Determination and Disarmament"

FACTOR LOADING	RESOLUTION	
INTERNATIONAL SECURITY—GENERAL (CONTINUED)		
0.86	47/46	AMENDMENT TREATY BANNING NUCLEAR TESTS
0.84	48/75c	GENERAL AND COMPLETE DISARMAMENT
0.79	46/34a	NUCLEAR CAPABILITY OF SOUTH AFRICA
0.76	46/36j	BILATERAL NUCLEAR-ARMS NEGOTIATIONS
0.69	48/68	VERIFICATION
PALESTINE		
0.89	46/46f	PALESTINE REFUGEES RATION DISTRIBUTION
0.86	47/64b	PALESTINE
0.86	47/69f	PALESTINE REFUGEES RATION DISTRIBUTION
0.86	46/74b	PALESTINE
0.86	46/74a	PALESTINE
0.86	46/46h	PALESTINE REFUGEES PROPERTY REVENUES
0.84	46/46g	RETURN POPULATION DISPLACED SINCE 1967
0.82	48/158b	PALESTINE
0.82	48/158a	PALESTINE
0.81	47/64a	PALESTINE
0.80	46/74c	PALESTINE
0.78	47/116f	SOUTH AFRICA–ISRAEL RELATIONS
0.77	46/79d	SOUTH AFRICA–ISRAEL RELATIONS
0.75	47/69h	PALESTINE REFUGEES PROPERTY REVENUES
0.74	47/69g	RETURN POPULATION DISPLACED SINCE 1967
0.73	48/158d	PALESTINE
0.73	46/82a	SITUATION IN THE MIDDLE EAST
0.69	46/75	INTERNATIONAL PEACE CONFERENCE MIDDLE EAST
0.69	48/40g	PALESTINIAN REFUGEES IN NEAR EAST
0.63	48/78	ISRAELI NUCLEAR ARMAMENT
0.62	47/64d	PALESTINE
0.62	46/47a	ISRAELI HUMAN RIGHTS PRACTICES
0.60	48/41a	ISRAELI HUMAN RIGHTS PRACTICES
0.58	47/70a	ISRAELI HUMAN RIGHTS PRACTICES
0.58	48/88	SITUATION IN BOSNIA AND HERZEGOVINA
0.53	47/121	SITUATION IN BOSNIA AND HERZEGOVINA
0.51	48/41d	ISRAELI HUMAN RIGHTS PRACTICES
0.50	48/41c	ISRAELI HUMAN RIGHTS PRACTICES

Voting Alignments in the General Assembly   37

independence movements, the United States has also been widely regarded as a neocolonial power. Its political position fairly high in the North (though not as high as France and the United Kingdom) is consistent with this perception. Similarly, the attention to disarmament concentrates on reducing the relative military power of all the Northern states. These issues had substantially defined the North-South conflict in earlier years, but had been conflated with the East-West confrontation when the Soviet Union and its East European allies voted quite regularly with the Southern states. Now the former communist states of the geographic north usually vote with the North, and a few developing countries have also shifted somewhat to the North. The North-South division now overwhelmingly defines the terms of political debate in the Assembly.

We can identify several of the big subissues related to the definition of the first "self-determination and disarmament" dimension in the post–Cold War period both by their high correlations with the dimension and their consistent salience across the three sessions (Table 3.1a). In the first group at the top of the table are various issues that can be characterized as condemning colonialism or neocolonialism. Heading it are several wide-ranging resolutions covering something of a grab bag of North-South issues. They all appeal for action on a spectrum of economic, social, and political matters, and especially for redressing inequalities. They include an effort to create an institute for the prevention of crime in Africa, calls for the liberation of remaining colonies, condemnation of the employment of mercenaries against liberation movements, specific condemnations of South Africa and apartheid, support for the Comoros Islands in a territorial dispute with France, assertion of a right to development and the indivisibility of human rights (Resolution 48/123), and calls for the restitution of cultural artifacts held in museums in the North. This collection of resolutions shows that the North-South divide is not merely over questions of distributive justice, but of political organization, morality, identity, and culture. In the second group are various calls for disarmament, resolutions sponsored by non-aligned countries to designate the Indian Ocean as a zone of peace, and other non-aligned supported resolutions condemning nuclear tests and directed against the major nuclear powers. The third group, labelled "Palestine," comprises many resolutions targeting Israel and, in the 47th and 48th sessions, two resolutions condemning Serbian aggression against the (largely Muslim) government of Bosnia. All these are issues on which the South was able to pile up reliable majorities.

TABLE 3.1B
Roll-Call Votes Correlated with "Political Rights" Factor
VARIANCE EXPLAINED: 10.8%

FACTOR LOADING		RESOLUTION
0.62	47/145	HUMAN RIGHTS IN IRAQ
0.62	47/146	HUMAN RIGHTS ISLAMIC REPUBLIC OF IRAN
0.57	48/131	PERIODIC AND GENUINE ELECTIONS
0.56	47/138	PERIODIC AND GENUINE ELECTIONS
0.55	46/86	RACISM AND RACIAL DISCRIMINATION
0.54	46/137	PERIODIC AND GENUINE ELECTIONS
0.52	48/147	SITUATION IN THE SUDAN
0.52	48/145	HUMAN RIGHTS ISLAMIC REPUBLIC OF IRAN
0.52	48/144	HUMAN RIGHTS IN IRAQ
0.52	46/134	HUMAN RIGHTS IN IRAQ

TABLE 3.1C
Roll-Call Votes Correlated with "Middle East"
VARIANCE EXPLAINED: 6.7%

FACTOR LOADING		RESOLUTION
0.57	48/212	ISRAELI SETTLEMENTS IN OCCUPIED TERR
0.54	47/172	ISRAELI SETTLEMENTS IN OCCUPIED TERR
0.54	46/199	ISRAELI SETTLEMENTS IN OCCUPIED TERR
0.52	47/64e	PALESTINE

Tables 3.1b and 3.1c show the factor patterns for the second and third major issue dimensions. The second dimension includes roll-call votes with high loadings on human rights questions in Iraq, Iran, and Sudan. It can be labeled, for the most part, a "political rights" dimension with an interventionist component, due to the high loadings both for resolutions that address problems in particular countries and for ones that call for increasing UN activities in providing assistance to countries in holding free and democratic elections. In this it contrasts with the first dimension's concentration on economic rights, anticolonialism, and great power military dominance. The high correlations of voting patterns on resolutions that consistently deal with human rights in particular

countries (chiefly Islamic ones), and on others that emphasize the importance of enhancing the effectiveness of periodic and genuine elections, single out this group as indicative of a distinct issue dimension unto itself. Criticisms of the three Islamic countries concentrate on violations of due process of law, arbitrary arrest, and torture. In these votes the Islamic countries and their allies lose. The third dimension, labeled "Middle East," is characterized by a few Arab-Israeli issues notable for the particular isolation of the United States and Israel in dissent from the Assembly majority. Here, as on the first dimension, the Islamic states are part of a larger majority.

Given these three underlying issue dimensions, what kinds of voting alignments can be found? Since our factor analysis delineates orthogonal dimensions that are uncorrelated with one another, the voting alignments for each dimension may be influenced by quite different economic, political, or cultural conditions. To illustrate the voting alignments of countries with respect to the separate issue dimensions, we divided countries into five major groups through a clustering routine.[9] These inductively derived groupings indicate which countries actually do vote in much the same way, unlike the caucusing groups, which may or may not exhibit similar voting behavior.

Table 3.2 shows countries in terms of their overall cluster membership. The first group, or cluster, includes the largest number of countries, almost exclusively from the NAM. The second and third clusters consist mainly of East as well as West European countries; the inclusion of Israel and the United States in the third cluster distinguishes the two voting groups. The fourth, also on the Western side, is a mixed cluster including Belarus, Russia, Ukraine, and several Pacific island countries. The fifth cluster comprises three countries—Malta, Republic of Korea, and Turkey—whose voting patterns are distinct enough to form a separate group.

Figure 3.1 illustrates the voting patterns of countries on the two most prominent dimensions. The vertical and horizontal axes display voting positions concerning the "self-determination" and "political rights" dimensions, respectively. Each country is denoted by the number of the cluster into which it falls (Table 3.2), and the clusters themselves are encircled. China and the United States are identified by name. The coordinates of each country's position are provided by factor scores, which are a weighted combination of factor loadings based on the correlation of each roll call with the latent issue dimension. Factor scores represent a composite measure of a country's voting position separately

TABLE 3.2

Cluster Membership of the General Assembly, 1991–93

CLUSTER 1:
NON-ALIGNED MOVEMENT

AFGHANISTAN
ALGERIA
ANGOLA
ANTIGUA AND BARBUDA
BAHAMAS
BAHRAIN
BANGLADESH
BARBADOS
BELIZE
BENIN
BHUTAN
BOLIVIA
BOTSWANA
BRAZIL
BRUNEI DARUSSALAM
BURKINA FASO
BURUNDI
CAMEROON
CAPE VERDE
CENTRAL AFRICAN REPUBLIC
CHAD
CHILE
CHINA
COLOMBIA
COMOROS
COSTA RICA
COTE D'LVOIRE
CUBA
CYPRUS
DEM PEOPLE'S REP OF KOREA
DJIBOUTI
DOMINICA
ECUADOR
EGYPT
EL SALVADOR
ETHIOPIA

FIJI
GABON
GAMBIA
GHANA
GUATEMALA
GUINEA
GUINEA-BISSAU
GUYANA
HAITI
HONDURAS
INDIA
INDONESIA
IRAN (ISLAMIC REPUBLIC)
IRAQ
JAMAICA
JORDAN
KENYA
KUWAIT
LAO PEOPLES' DEM REPUBLIC
LEBANON
LESOTHO
LIBYAN ARAB JAMAHIRIYA
MADAGASCAR
MALAWI
MALAYSIA
MALDIVES
MALI
MAURITANIA
MAURITIUS
MEXICO
MONGOLIA
MOROCCO
MOZAMBIQUE
MYANMAR
NAMIBIA
NEPAL

NICARAGUA
NIGER
NIGERIA
OMAN
PAKISTAN
PANAMA
PAPUA NEW GUINEA
PARAGUAY
PERU
PHILIPPINES
QATAR
RWANDA
SAUDI ARABIA
SENEGAL
SIERRA LEONE
SINGAPORE
SRI LANKA
ST. VINCENT & GRENADINES
ST. LUCIA
SUDAN
SURINAME
SWAZILAND
SYRIAN ARAB REPUBLIC
THAILAND
TOGO
TRINIDAD AND TOBAGO
TUNISIA
UGANDA
UNITED ARAB EMIRATES
UNITED REP OF TANZANIA
VENEZUELA
VIETNAM
YEMEN
ZAMBIA
ZIMBABWE

TABLE 3.2 (CONTINUED)
Cluster Membership
of the General Assembly, 1991–93

CLUSTER 2: EUROPE, JAPAN

ARGENTINA	GREECE	NEW ZEALAND
AUSTRALIA	ICELAND	NORWAY
AUSTRIA	IRELAND	POLAND
CZECH REPUBLIC	JAPAN	PORTUGAL
DENMARK	LATVIA	SPAIN
ESTONIA	LIECHTENSTEIN	SWEDEN
FINLAND	LITHUANIA	

CLUSTER 3: EUROPE, US, ISRAEL

BELGIUM	HUNGARY	ROMANIA
BULGARIA	ISRAEL	UNITED KINGDOM
CANADA	ITALY	UNITED STATES
FRANCE	LUXEMBOURG	
GERMANY	NETHERLANDS	

CLUSTER 4: RUSSIA, EASTERN EUROPE, OTHERS

BELARUS	RUSSIAN FEDERATION	URUGUAY
MARSHALL ISLANDS	SAMOA	
MICRONESIA (FED STATES)	UKRAINE	

CLUSTER 5: MALTA, SOUTH KOREA, TURKEY

MALTA	REPUBLIC OF KOREA	TURKEY

for each of the self-determination and political rights dimensions, taking into account both how the individual country voted on all the resolutions contributing to the particular issue dimensions and how strongly each resolution itself is correlated with the larger issue dimension. States that regularly voted against self-determination resolutions have high negative scores and thus are located on the "northern" end of the vertical axis; states that most often supported such resolutions have positive scores and thus are located in the "south." Similarly for the horizontal

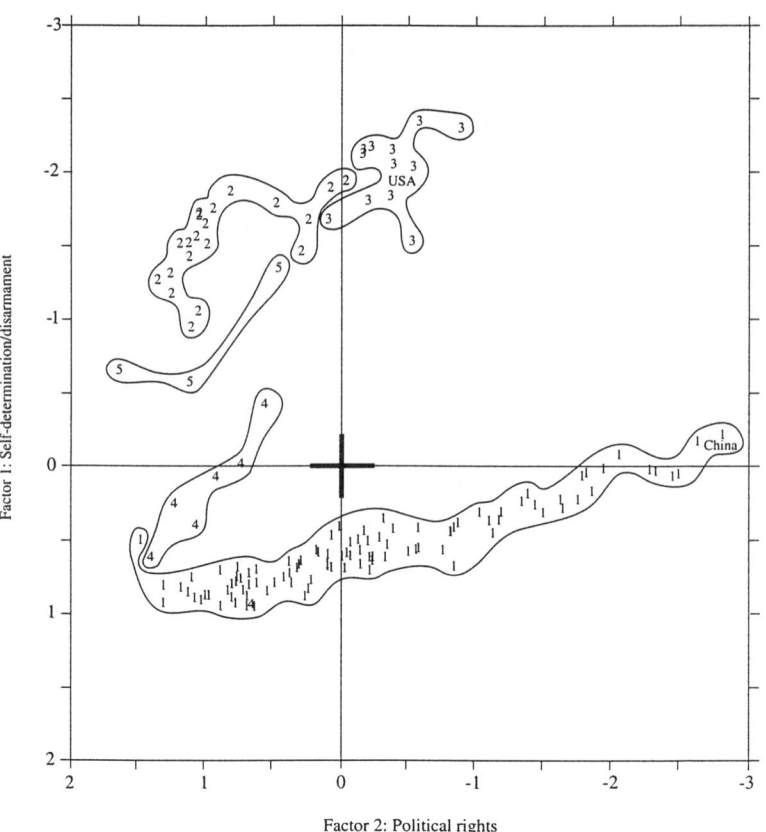

FIGURE 3.1: Grouping in the General Assembly, 1991–93

axis, states that regularly voted in favor of interventionist resolutions upholding political rights are located by their positive scores on the left ("western") side, and those that most often resisted passage of such resolutions have negative scores to the "east." The distribution along the two dimensions reveals the major voting groups.

On the self-determination dimension alone, countries are bifurcated largely along North-South lines, with the only fourth cluster, which includes Russia, and the anomalous fifth cluster forming a rather sparse middle ground. Note, too, that the countries of the North are spread over a larger vertical space than are countries of the South, which are positioned in a much more cohesive manner on this vertical dimension. Despite the number and diversity of subissues representing the first issue dimension, most countries divide rather neatly into two distinct groups. The second issue dimension, however, represented by political rights questions, yields a less clear-cut delineation of cohesive groups of countries. In particular, the countries of the South are distributed much more widely along the horizontal axis. The fourth cluster, which includes Russia, votes as part of the West on these issues. In general, countries' preferences on general questions of self-determination seem largely defined by strata of economic development, while country-specific questions of political rights appear to reflect more diverse influences. The Middle East dimension (not graphed) shows substantial agreement among the vast majority of countries. Israel and the United States are quite isolated. In contrast to their spread on the second dimension, the NAM countries exhibit relatively cohesive voting behavior on the Middle East dimension.

The factor scores are also useful indicators of alienation from the majority on both dimensions. When each country is weighted according to its relative distance from the focal point of the "compass," the mean or center of gravity of the General Assembly is precisely at the zero point where the two directional axes meet, marked by a dark cross. However, the scale is more truncated south of the horizontal axis than it is to the north—indicating that the majority of states are in the south and that those in outlying positions tend to be found in the far north (e.g., the United States). Similarly, the scale is more truncated to the west than to the east, with the "extremists" like China usually in the east. The modal point—that is, the point that divides the members of the General Assembly exactly in half—lies in the southwest quadrant, not too far from the point where the horizontal and vertical axes cross. This reflects the fact that most resolutions that come to vote in the General Assembly pass.

The recent dominance of a North-South division reflects a major change in the way countries manifest their preferences with respect to the content and salience of issues chosen to define security. Earlier, the North-South division was always far overshadowed by an East-West division that accounted for a much larger proportion of roll-call votes. The strengthening of this North-South division in light of the end of the Cold War is not surprising. But its encompassing nature is impressive: it explained five times the variance of any other dimension.

We believe that these voting alignments rather accurately reflect the issues and the economic and political influences on state alignments not only in the General Assembly but also in the wider arena of world politics more generally. (We present some evidence for this in the next section.) But do the alignments also reflect the relative *power* of states to achieve their goals in the wider arena of world politics? In many respects they clearly do not. On self-determination and disarmament issues, for example, the South can consistently produce large voting majorities, but neither outside the UN nor in the General Assembly itself do southern countries have great power to enforce the resolutions they pass. Nevertheless, they continue to introduce and pass such resolutions as a means of exerting moral suasion on the North, with some success. The North usually cannot prevent these issues from being put on the agenda, and often can do little more than dilute the wording of successful resolutions. Yet the West frequently is able to introduce, and to pass, resolutions upholding basic political rights violated by particular developing countries. Different groups of states are able not only to be heard, but also to assemble majorities on different kinds of issues that represent critical fault lines of global politics.

To illustrate the changes in voting alignments from the height of the Cold War era we replicated the analysis above for General Assembly sessions 38 through 40 (1983-85).[10] The clustering routine for this period produced four groups of states, rather than five as for sessions 46 through 48; Table 3.3 presents a list of countries and their cluster memberships.

The four clusters represent (1) the NAM, (2) Western Europe and Japan, (3) Western Europe, Israel and the United States, and (4) the Soviet bloc. The first three clusters correspond closely to the groupings we observed in the most recent sessions. The composition of the non-aligned group is quite consistent, and the two European groups also show marked continuity. As in the previous clustering results, the two West European clusters are distinguished by the extent of countries' agreement with the United States and Israel on Middle East issues. The first of them, including Japan, more clearly than before is composed substantially of the traditional European neutral countries and a number of smaller European or European-settled states. The second comprises the United States and many of its closest and more reliable allies, including Canada, France, Germany, and the United Kingdom. The Soviet bloc—then including Eastern Europe—shows a great deal of solidarity, though not quite as much as in earlier Cold War years, when little daylight appeared between the voting positions of any members. By the 1990s, of course, this bloc had collapsed, with Cuba, Laos, Mongolia, and Vietnam going with the NAM, most of Eastern Europe

TABLE 3.3
Cluster Membership of the General Assembly, 1983–85

CLUSTER 1: NON-ALIGNED MOVEMENT

ALGERIA	GREECE	PARAGUAY
ANGOLA	GUATEMALA	PERU
ARGENTINA	GUINEA	PHILIPPINES
BAHAMAS	GUINEA-BISSAU	QATAR
BAHRAIN	GUYANA	ROMANIA
BANGLADESH	HAITI	RWANDA
BARBADOS	HONDURAS	SAO TOME & PRINCIPE
BENIN	INDIA	
BHUTAN	INDONESIA	SAUDI ARABIA
BOLIVIA	IRAN	SENEGAL
BOTSWANA	IRAQ	SIERRA LEONE
BRAZIL	IVORY COAST	SINGAPORE
BURKINA FASO	JAMAICA	SOMALIA
BURMA	JORDAN	SOMOA
BURUNDI	KENYA	SRI LANKA
CAMBODIA	KUWAIT	ST. LUCIA
CAMEROON	LEBANON	SUDAN
CAPE VERDE	LESOTHO	SURINAME
CENTRAL AFRICAN REPUBLIC	LIBERIA	SWAZILAND
	LIBYA	SYRIA
CHAD	MADAGASCAR	TANZANIA
CHILE	MALAWI	THAILAND
CHINA	MALAYSIA	TOGO
COLOMBIA	MALDIVES	TRINIDAD AND TOBAGO
CONGO	MALI	
COSTA RICA	MALTA	TUNISIA
CYPRUS	MAURITANIA	TURKEY
DJIBOUTI	MAURITIUS	UGANDA
DOMINICAN REPUBLIC	MEXICO	UNITED ARAB EMIRATES
	MOROCCO	
ECUADOR	MOZAMBIQUE	URUGUAY
EGYPT	NEPAL	VENEZUELA
EL SALVADOR	NICARAGUA	YEMEN ARAB REPUBLIC
EQUATORIAL GUINEA	NIGER	
	NIGERIA	YEMEN PEOPLES' REPUBLIC
ETHIOPIA	OMAN	
FIJI	PAKISTAN	YUGOSLAVIA
GABON	PANAMA	ZAIRE
GAMBIA	PAPAU NEW GUINEA	ZAMBIA
GHANA		ZIMBABWE

TABLE 3.3 (CONTINUED)
Cluster Membership of the General Assembly, 1983–85

CLUSTER 2: EUROPE, JAPAN

AUSTRALIA	FINLAND	NORWAY
AUSTRIA	ICELAND	PORTUGAL
DENMARK	JAPAN	SPAIN
	NEW ZEALAND	SWEDEN

CLUSTER 3: EUROPE, US, ISRAEL

BELGIUM	GERMAN FEDERAL REPUBLIC	ITALY
CANADA		LUXEMBOURG
FRANCE	ISRAEL	NETHERLANDS

CLUSTER 4: SOVIET BLOC

AFGHANISTAN	GERMAN DEMOCRATIC REPUBLIC	POLAND
BELARUS		SOVIET UNION
BULGARIA	HUNGARY	UKRAINE
CUBA	LAOS	VIETNAM
CZECHOSLOVAKIA	MONGOLIA	

aligning with other Europeans, and Belarus, Russia, and Ukraine somewhat distinct but definitely in the northwest quadrant.

Figure 3.2 shows how the clusters were distributed on the two major voting dimensions. The first, graphed on the vertical axis, combined elements of issues that characterized both East-West and North-South divisions. Accounting for 42.8 percent of all the variance, it incorporates votes on aspects of development, South Africa and Namibia, colonialism, nuclear and other disarmament issues, and Israeli policies toward Palestinians. As during earlier Cold War years, these were issues on which the Assembly majority "voting machine" regularly defeated the democracies of the North and West. But very striking was the virtual coincidence of the "non-aligned" states with the Soviet bloc on the great majority of these issues. A simple East-West image of Cold War bipolarity was never very accurate, or very informative.

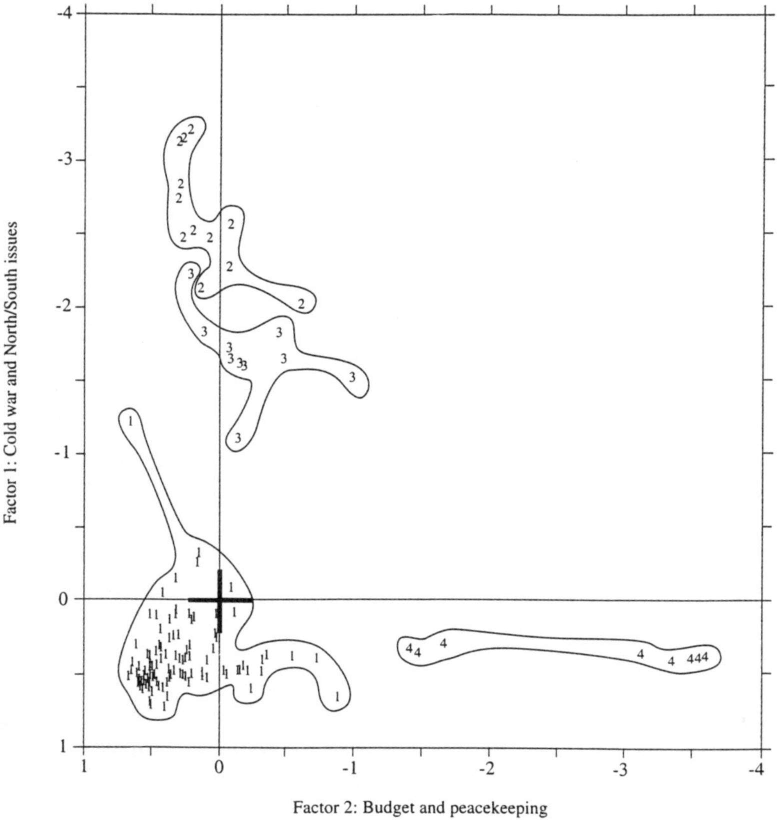

Voting Alignments in the General Assembly 47

FIGURE 3.2: Groupings in the General Assembly, 1983–85

The Soviet Union and its allies, however, were not always in the majority. On various disarmament issues relating to weapons of mass destruction, Japan and many West European nations, including the Scandinavian countries, split from other Europeans to vote with the majority against both the Soviet bloc and the close allies of the United States. And on a substantial number of votes on financing the United Nations, for the program budget and especially for some peacekeeping activities, the Soviet bloc was consistently in the minority. The Cold War still produced votes indicative of some very clear divisions between East and West on which the West did not lose. In the most notable of these, the vast majority of non-aligned countries joined to condemn

Soviet actions in Afghanistan. As a group, these issues delineate the second rotated factor, explaining 12.2 percent of the variance, graphed along the horizontal axis. Along the vertical axis the Soviet bloc voted exclusively with the NAM, but along the horizontal axis most of the South regularly joined the West in voting against the Soviet bloc.

Caucusing Groups and Political-Economic Influences

In addition to the inductively derived voting groups, we can also identify the degree to which actual voting alignments correspond to the positions of various recognized "regional" caucusing groups in the United Nations. States form these groups so as to secure regional representation, and, by encouraging solidarity in voting, to maximize the groups' influence over outcomes. In practice, groups vary widely in their ability to do so. Figure 3.3 lists these groups; note that there is some overlap of groups. Israel is not a member of any caucusing group. The United States is included among the Western Europe and other states group, but it caucuses with them only for election purposes. Table 3.4 presents the correlations of the factor scores for members of each group with the first two voting dimensions in the 46th through the 48th sessions. (Since the third dimension is marked mainly by the isolation of the United States and Israel it is of less interest.)

On the self-determination dimension, the so-called Group of 77 (now much larger) and the NAM, with high positive correlations, and Western Europe (including the United States) and to a lesser extent the European Community, with high negative correlations, have the most divergent voting positions. For the political rights dimension, we can identify no high association for any caucusing group, though the Latin American and Caribbean group, with many new democratic regimes, shows the greatest support for political rights resolutions. Most groups are fairly near the mean on this dimension, and many show sharply divergent voting patterns within themselves. The final two columns give the mean and standard deviation for each group's factor scores; the standard deviation constitutes an index of the group's dispersion. The mere existence of a caucusing group hardly insures uniform voting behavior.[11] Two large groups, the African and Arab ones, however, are very cohesive on self-determination and disarmament issues. In the General Assembly, unlike the Security Council, which privileges veto-wielding great powers,

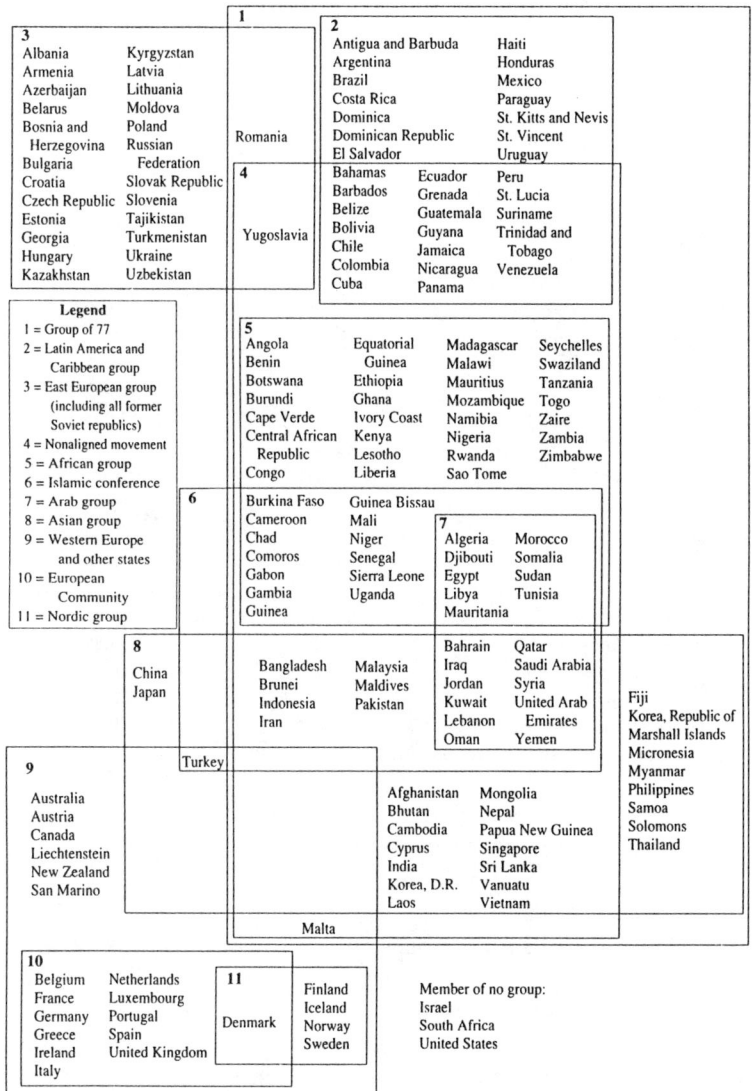

FIGURE 3.3: Overlapping Caucusing Groups in the United Nations as of January 1993
Source. Adapted with permission of the publisher from Robert E. Riggs and Jack C. Plano, *The United Nations* (Belmont, CA: Wadsworth, 1994, 2nd ed.), p. 62

TABLE 3.4
Factor Scores and Caucusing Groups*

CAUCUSING GROUP	SELF-DETERMINATION		
	Correlation	Mean	Std. Dev.
Western Europe and other states**	-0.73	-1.73	0.42
European Community	-0.58	-1.95	0.36
Eastern European Group	-0.36	-1.28	0.83
Nordic Group	-0.33	-1.69	0.08
Asian Group	0.14	0.29	0.55
Arab Group	0.17	0.46	0.25
Islamic Conference	0.25	0.43	0.36
African Group	0.34	0.52	0.21
Latin America & Caribbean Group	0.39	0.71	0.39
Non-Aligned Movement	0.67	0.52	0.30
Group of 77	0.89	0.50	0.41

CAUCUSING GROUP	POLITICAL RIGHTS		
	Correlation	Mean	Std. Dev.
African Group	-0.31	-0.38	0.81
Non-Aligned Movement	-0.31	-0.25	0.99
Islamic Conference	-0.28	-0.44	0.85
Asian Group	-0.21	-0.35	1.18
Group of 77	-0.16	-0.10	1.02
Arab Group	-0.16	-0.48	0.97
European Community	0.05	0.22	0.79
Eastern European Group	0.09	0.38	0.60
Nordic Group	0.17	0.85	0.34
Western Europe and other states**	0.22	0.49	0.76
Latin America & Caribbean Group	0.36	0.59	0.77

*Adapted from Figure 3.3
**United States caucuses with this group for election purposes

large and cohesive caucusing groups can exert substantial power to block resolutions, and to pass them. On the second dimension only one small group (the Nordic group) is at all cohesive.

The prominence of a North-South split in voting alignments raises three important questions about the evolution of voting preferences among General Assembly members. First, since such a division appears important on the self-determination issue dimension, we hypothesize that voting preferences will in fact be strongly correlated with states' average income levels, measured by per capita gross national product

(GNP). Second, we may ask whether the greater proportion of democracies among states, manifested both in changes in former communist states and in developing countries, is reflected in clear voting divisions between political system types; namely, between democratic regimes and those authoritarian ones that remain. Such a hypothesis follows from the observation that democracies tend to ally with one another, and seems even more pertinent to issues of political rights than to the issues comprising the self-determination dimension.[12] Finally, it seems likely that economic ties with the United States should affect the degree to which states tend to vote with that power. Economic ties, however, might affect votes in two very different ways. Two competing hypotheses are plausible and may affect each dimension differently. One hypothesis is that, especially on self-determination issues, close economic integration with the U.S. market (measured as a state's trade with the U.S. as a share of that state's GNP) may, *ceteris paribus,* produce or exacerbate sentiments of economic exploitation ("dependencia") that would produce strong voting divergence from the United States and other Northern states. The other is that trade with the United States may produce or reflect similar voting alignments by liberal states, perhaps especially on issues of political rights.

To test these hypotheses we employ a statistical model (multiple regression) that allows us to measure the effect of each independent variable while holding the others constant, with voting positions along the two issue dimensions as dependent variables.[13] Table 3.5 shows the results of this analysis. The first column for each issue dimension shows the regression coefficient for each independent variable, and the second shows the value of a t-test for statistical significance. The higher the t-value the stronger the relationship.

GNP per capita, democracy, and trade with the United States all are associated, with high statistical significance (.001 level), with voting positions on the self-determination dimension. Negative coefficients for GNP per capita and democracy indicate that countries with higher values on these variables tended to vote together against resolutions backed and usually passed by the South. In contrast, the positive coefficient for trade with the United States indicates that—once one has controlled for the independent effects of wealth and democracy that produce a tilt toward Northern voting—countries that trade more with the United States tend to vote with the South, as could be expected on a dimension emphasizing development.

For the political rights dimension, two of the three explanatory variables are again statistically significant, but together they prove

TABLE 3.5
Predictors of Issue Positions

	SELF-DETERMINATION		POLITICAL RIGHTS	
	Estimate	t	Estimate	t
GNP per capita	-7.40	-7.86	0.74	0.67
Democracy	-0.38	-3.80	0.51	4.41
Trade with U.S.	2.53	5.20	1.14	2.02
Adjusted R-squared	0.55		0.20	
Number of countries	128		128	

much less powerful than for the first dimension. GNP per capita makes little difference on political rights resolutions. Higher levels of trade with the United States, however, are positively correlated (.01 level) with votes critical of countries' rights record, as is democracy (and even more strongly) when we control for trade and income level.[14] Note that democracies vote very similarly on both dimensions—despite the fact that the issues in question are largely quite different from those that ostensibly brought them together in their Cold War–generated alliances.

When we analyze these results in terms of caucusing groups, we find that Western Europe, the European Community, and the Nordic group all tend to vote with the United States against self-determination resolutions even though they may conduct a great deal of trade with the United States. The same is true of Eastern Europe. Europe has no history of dependencia; to the contrary. Of the various regionally defined caucusing groups of the South, however, the one most strongly aligned in favor of self-determination resolutions is the Latin American and Caribbean group. (See Table 3.4.)

These voting patterns in the General Assembly help to illuminate the influences on state alignments in other UN bodies, notably the Security Council. Figure 3.4 maps the General Assembly voting patterns of Security Council members during the 1993 and 1994 sessions. These patterns, of course, may not be present in actual Security Council votes. The composition of the two bodies is very different, as are their voting rules. With the Security Council operating on a near-consensus basis in

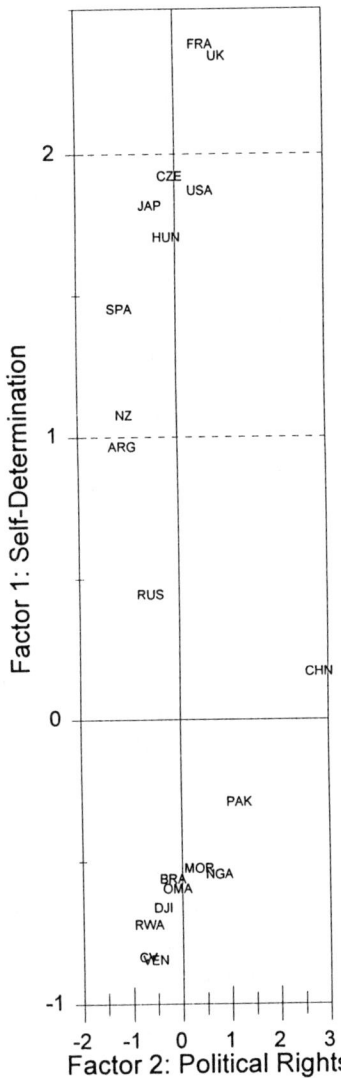

FIGURE 3.4: Security Council Members, 1993–94
Voting Patterns in the General Assembly

recent years, actual voting patterns there would tell us relatively little about underlying disagreements. Moreover, issues under consideration by the Security Council at any given time cannot be considered by the General Assembly at the same time. Even so, issues do, substantively and ideologically, overlap. We have therefore projected voting patterns from the General Assembly onto the latent, if not the manifest, divisions in the Security Council in Figure 3.4. We have contracted the scale on the horizontal axis to one-fifth that of the vertical axis. We do this to reflect the proportionately far greater influence of the self-determination dimension in determining countries' voting alignments across the full range of Assembly resolutions.

Of the 1993 Security Council members, France, Hungary, Japan, New Zealand, Russia, Spain, the United Kingdom, and the United States formed one major grouping, while another consisted of Brazil, China, Cape Verde, Djibouti, Morocco, Pakistan, and Venezuela. In 1994 two new members, Argentina and the Czech Republic, joined the group in the northwest quadrant, replacing Hungary and Japan. Nigeria, Oman, and Rwanda replaced Cape Verde, Morocco, and Venezuela in the South. In both years, the Security Council members' General Assembly voting patterns indicate a division into two groups of eight and seven. The first group appears less cohesive than the second, with the greatest distance separating Russia and France. The second group finds all seven countries positioned closely together along the vertical axis. The pattern of groupings shows, as observed above for the full General Assembly, that for the wide spectrum of issues regarding self-determination, states are polarized into two main groups, roughly dividing countries into North and South.

Overall, four of the five permanent members of the Security Council are not too far apart, with Russia at some distance from France, the United Kingdom, and the United States. But China is very distant from all the others. The first three, and Russia to a lesser extent, usually can depend on having allies among the other permanent members. While the alignments may be much the same in the two bodies, the results are not. Because of their veto power, the four can dominate the Security Council to a greater degree than they can the much larger General Assembly. China, because it is so politically distant from the other permanent members, must depend in the Security Council on its ability to wield a veto against a resolution that offends it, whereas in the General Assembly it has many reliable allies.

Continuity and Change

We have addressed several questions regarding the voting patterns of the United Nations General Assembly: What are the underlying issue dimensions reflected in the resolutions put to roll-call votes? How do member states align themselves with respect to these dimensions? How can we characterize those states, and what implications do the characterizations have for political processes in the United Nations? Our analysis focused primarily on three post–Cold War sessions of the General Assembly, but we were also able to compare those patterns characteristic of earlier years.

With the end of the Cold War, voting patterns in the General Assembly reflect the erosion of the East-West division that had dominated much of United Nations activities. Left behind as major foci are many issues relating to the self-determination of colonized peoples, and, to a lesser extent, questions of political rights within states. During the Cold War era, when many "non-aligned" states regularly voted with the Soviet bloc, the modal point of the General Assembly often was found in the southeast quadrant. It is now somewhat to the southwest. Four of the five permanent members of the Security Council, however, are in the northwest quadrant, suggesting their current ability to hold that body on a very different course from the Assembly.

The North-South split now characterizes voting positions as much as the East-West split once did. The importance of North-South issues is not new, but during the Cold War years it tended to be conflated with and overshadowed by East-West issues as a source of division.[15] The resurgence of North-South voting renews and strengthens a long-standing alignment, one now likely to dominate the United Nations for a substantial time to come. Voting alignments are likely to be shaped by state preferences along developmental lines, and views of self-determination and economic development will reflect the continuing great differences between rich and poor nations.

NOTES

1. Hayward R. Alker, Jr., "Dimensions of Conflict in the General Assembly," *American Political Science Review* 58 (1964), pp. 642-57.

2. Alker identified voting alignments according to the unrotated factor matrix, which captures the *behavioral* aspect of General Assembly voting by maximizing the variance explained by the first factor. The first factor of the unrotated solution thus identifies the collection of issues on which agreements and disagreements, in the form of voting alignments, arise most clearly and frequently in states' voting behavior. The rotated factor matrix, in contrast, captures the *substantive* aspect of General Assembly voting behavior by identifying the latent issue dimensions underlying clusters of resolutions that correlate most highly with each factor.

3. Hayward R. Alker, Jr., and Bruce Russett, *World Politics in the General Assembly* (New Haven: Yale University Press, 1965).

4. Bruce Russett, "Discovering Voting Groups in the United Nations," *American Political Science Review* 50 (1966), pp. 327-39; Bruce Russett, *International Regions and the International System: A Study in Political Ecology* (Chicago: Rand McNally, 1967).

5. Hanna Newcombe, Michael Ross, and Alan G. Newcombe, "United Nations Voting Patterns," *International Organization* 24 (1970), pp. 100-121; Richard Powers, "United Nations Voting Alignments: A New Equilibrium," *Western Political Quarterly* 33 (1980), pp. 167-84.

6. Steven Holloway, "Forty Years of United Nations General Assembly Voting," *Canadian Journal of Political Science* 23 (1990), pp. 279-96; Steven Holloway and Rodney Tomlinson, "The New World Order and the General Assembly: Bloc Realignment at the UN in the Post - Cold War Period," *Canadian Journal of Political Science* 28 (1995), pp. 227-54 subsequently extended this analysis to 1991, with results compatible to what we show below for up to 1993. A new analytical model confirms the utility of factor analysis in analyzing roll-call voting. See James Heckman and James Snyder, "A Latent Factor Model of Voting" (Economics Department, University of Chicago, 1995, manuscript).

7. Following Alker and Russett, we defined voting preferences—yes, abstain, and no—as an ordinal scale. A movement from abstain to yes or no is considered one shift, while a movement from yes to no, or vice versa, is considered two shifts. Resolutions that passed with the minority voting within ten shifts of a unanimous vote were excluded from the analysis. This exclusion rule avoids the addition of redundant information regarding the extent of agreement and highlights the delineation of the major voting groups. In practice, this ten-shift rule excludes fewer roll calls recently than it did in the Alker-Russett period, when the membership of the General Assembly was about half its current size. Ranking the votes according to the number of countries voting in each category serves to differentiate the preferences reflected by, for example, a single no vote against an overwhelming majority voting otherwise. In this case the distribution of the rankings (by z-scores) would be wider than for a more evenly distributed set of votes.

8. Three factors were extracted by (1) using Guttman's weakest lower bound of employing unities as initial communality estimates and extracting factors with eigenvalues greater than or equal to one ; and (2) using the discontinuity criterion, which posits that eigenvalues, as depicted in scree plots, will show a

sharp discontinuity after the last substantively important factor has been extracted and then show a fairly constant slope as the number of factors increases. See R. J. Rummel, *Applied Factor Analysis* (Evanston: Northwestern University Press, 1970), pp. 357-58, 364. In this analysis, the drop in eigenvalues, followed by a leveling out, occurred following the extraction of the third factor. In subsequent factors the small number of roll-call votes loading on any of the subsequent factors did not impart a clear substantive interpretation. Percentages of variance accounted for by the three rotated factors are, respectively, 50.5 percent, 10.8 percent, and 6.7 percent.

9. In this case, the routine enables a grouping of countries using a similarity measure based on the closeness of countries' voting patterns. The clustering procedure used a nearest centroid sorting method designed to minimize the sum of square distances from the cluster means. Similarity measures were Euclidean distances computed from coordinate data. Clustering into four and six groups produced less substantively interpretable results. This method and results are very similar to those in the next chapter, by Barry O'Neill.

10. This analysis, with exclusion rules applied, included 344 resolutions, more than twice that for the 46th through 48th sessions. This reflects a continuation of what others have noted as the tendency of the General Assembly in recent years (1) to adopt more resolutions without vote, and (2) to have more unanimous roll-call votes. See Miguel Marín-Bosch, "How Nations Vote in the General Assembly of the United Nations," *International Organization* 41 (1987), pp. 705-24.

11. See M. J. Peterson, *The General Assembly in World Politics* (Boston: Allen and Unwin, 1986), pp. 291-97.

12. Randolph Siverson and Julianne Emmons, "Birds of a Feather: Democratic Political Systems and Alliance Choices," *Journal of Conflict Resolution* 35 (1991), pp. 285-306.

13. Democracy data were obtained from the Harvey Starr and Michael Gubser revision of data from Freedom House Data in Raymond D. Gastil, *Freedom in the World: Political Rights and Civil Liberties, 1988 - 1989* (New York: Freedom House, 1989), and subsequent editions. Trade data are from the *Direction of Trade Statistics Yearbook, 1994*. GNP and GNP per capita are from the *World Bank Atlas, 1993, 1994, and 1995*. Values were averaged for the 1991-93 period. GNP per capita figures are in ten-thousand-dollar units. Belgium represents both Belgium and Luxembourg in the regression analysis because the trade data combine the two countries into one trading unit.

14. Multicollinearity is probably not a major problem in that the correlation between democracy and GNP per capita is only 0.45, and correlations between those two and trade with the United States are even smaller (0.14 and -0.05 respectively).

15. See Alker and Russett, *World Politics in the General Assembly*.

4

POWER AND SATISFACTION IN THE SECURITY COUNCIL

BARRY O'NEILL

How could the Security Council be made more equitable? One way would be to include all 185 states, from China to Palau, and give them all one vote. This kind of equity is not what advocates of revision have in mind, of course; the Council was never intended to duplicate the General Assembly. In the context of the Security Council, equity does not mean straight equality, but representation in proportion to some appropriate degree. Much of the current debate over redesigning the Security Council involves just what features of a country merit giving it a Council role. Should it be given a seat on the basis of its population, or perhaps that of its region? A country's influence in world affairs might count, so that decisions taken by the Council will be those that the world community can stand behind. Should membership be based in part on the country's financial contribution, or its military capabilities? Should it require that a state have a record of following United Nations principles?

Criteria for representation give only half the answer to questions about redesigning the Council. The other part involves measuring the power that a given voting scheme confers. In the present Council, for example, states with vetoes hold more voting power than the others, but how much more? What would happen to a veto member's voting power if the rules were changed, for example, by adding more seats or altering the requirement for a majority? This chapter addresses the second problem, and will discuss how to measure the degree of power conveyed by a certain voting scheme, and how satisfied a state can be with its voting power. It looks at the logical consequences of certain voting rules and describes a measure of each country's resulting voting power. It uses the *Shapley-Shubik index,* a formal way to measure the power accruing to a voter proposed by Lloyd Shapley and Martin Shubik in 1954.[1] In their measure, each member of a voting body receives a certain share or percentage of the total power, a number that one can calculate from the voting rules.

Questions about measuring voting power in turn raise deeper issues of the nature of power. How does voting power fit in with other sources of power in world affairs? A general theory of power has been a persistent problem in political science. The concept has been regarded as central and sometimes has been elevated to an almost metaphysical status, a commodity that determines success in conflicts but can never be fully defined. Robert Dahl[2] took a more down-to-earth view, stating that power is the probability that one party can change another's behavior; that is, the probability it can get the other to do what it might not have done otherwise.

Dahl's work did not directly influence Shapley and Shubik, but their approach was consistent with his, and Straffin[3] later clarified the connection. Within Dahl's framework, Shapley and Shubik are estimating the likelihood that a voting member will be able to get the whole legislature to do what the member wants, judging by only one basis of power, the member's formal role in the rules of voting. Straffin showed that the Shapley-Shubik index is the power (in Dahl's sense) of the individual over the voting body, the likelihood that the body would respond to a change of preference by the individual, based on certain assumptions of the kind of issues that arise and how the members vote. Straffin's assumptions are that votes occur in the following way, a model that we will term the *basic model of voting.* A resolution is proposed to the voting body. Some number p is chosen randomly, with all values between 0 and 1 equally likely. Each member votes for the resolution with probability p or against it with probability $1-p$. This p could be viewed as the overall popularity of the resolution. Each member's vote, yes or no, is independent of the others' votes, conditional on the value of p—given that we know p, learning how one member will vote tells us nothing more about how another will vote. A member's power is the probability that changing its vote will change the outcome in the same way—that the member's yes vote will pass the resolution and the member's no vote will reject it. The members' powers defined in this way sum to 1, so it makes sense to think about them as proportions of the total power.[4]

In certain simple cases where a member's power is obvious, the Shapley-Shubik index gives the proper results. For example, if all members have equal votes then all are assigned equal powers, or if one is a dictator then that person gets a Shapley-Shubik power of 1, or if one member can make no difference to the outcome of any vote the individual is assigned a power of 0. In other applications where the results are not obvious, the Shapley-Shubik index gives reasonable values. It can be calculated for any kind of assembly that has well-defined voting rules, e.g., for those that assign different voting weights to their members and require a certain total weight to pass a resolution, or for multicameral legislatures where a resolution has to pass a sequence of houses to succeed. It is usually easy to calculate even for large voting bodies, as long as the voting rules are not too intricate.

Other measures of voting power have been proposed.[5] The main competitor is generally regarded as the Banzhaf index, but I believe the Shapley-Shubik index has the most desirable properties in the particular context of the Security Council. A rationale for the Banzhaf index following Straffin's approach involves an assumption that each person votes for or against a motion with probability ½, all independent of the others. The independence assumption seems unreasonable. Knowing that most members will vote for a resolution should increase our expectation that a further member will vote for it, and the rationale behind the Shapley-Shubik index includes this feature.

The definition of voting power as the probability of making a difference, given a simple model, shows that it is only one component of overall power—that conferred by the voting rules. Other bases of power on the Council, such as the benefits of a charismatic ambassador to the UN, or the possession of resources to induce others to support you, are not considered. Nor does the measure include the fact that membership in the Council conveys power outside it, for example, by granting prestige or access to information. (Of course a Security Council seat might sometimes be a liability, as Yemen discovered when it was pressured by both sides over the 1991 Gulf War. Much of the current ambivalence in Japan involves the worry that membership will come with an expectation of a greater role in military activities.) These considerations are important, but the question of overall power is too complex to solve at once—a better approach is to take a single step at a time. Power conveyed by a right to vote is the easiest to measure since voting rules are typically well-defined, and it holds a number of surprises. The work here lies in a tradition of formal analyses of voting that goes back at least to the eighteenth century. The goal is not to define an optimal voting scheme, but to set up a system that helps us think clearly about voting rules and power.[6]

The analysis presented here differs from past work in three ways: it looks at certain recent suggestions for changes, it asks how "satisfied" states will be with their power in a sense to be defined, and most importantly it takes account of common interests likely to arise among states, which have a great effect on their measured power.

The first section analyzes current Council rules and points out some consequences of small changes. The next section considers the satisfaction conferred by having a vote. This concept is related to power but not identical to it. A country can have no vote, but feel satisfied with its decisions if it has allies on the Council who make sure its interests are protected. Dissatisfaction can occur either when the Council passes resolutions that the state does not want or when the Council rejects resolutions that the state favors. Current proposals for revision tend to increase the latter outcome—with more vetoes, some state or other is more able to block a popular resolution. The second section asks whether certain revision proposals might obstruct the Council's effectiveness, so that adding veto members might mean that the Council would be unable to respond in a crisis.

The third section takes account of continuing alliances among states. These alliances might arise by deliberate plan, such as the non-aligned bloc that arose in the middle 1950s, or they might be naturally induced by national interests where similar states simply tend to vote in the same way. The likelihood is high, for example, that Saudi Arabia and the United Arab Emirates will find themselves on the same side of a debate, or that Western industrialized countries like the United States and Britain will be together. The basic Shapley-Shubik index does not consider this phenomenon, as it is based only on the abstract rules of voting. The basic model makes one state's vote independent of another's conditional on the resolution's overall popularity p. Various modifications to the index allow us to include likely common interests.[7]

A simple example shows how natural alliances can change the distribution of power. Imagine a voting body of three states where each state has a single vote. Barring other considerations their power would be equal. However, if two of the three regularly combined together, these two would have a voting majority and complete control, and the third state would become powerless. The power distribution had been (⅓, ⅓, ⅓), but with the alliance it changes to (½, ½, 0). The third section looks at the new patterns that have emerged since the end of the Cold War, based on voting data from the 46th, 47th, and 48th General Assembly sessions, as developed by Kim and Russett in chapter three.

Voting Power without Continuing Alliances

Shapley-Shubik indices calculated for the 1995 Security Council and some imaginary ones like it are shown in Table 4.1. I assume there are no abstentions—the effect of these will be introduced later.

A striking result of these calculations is the tiny power of the nonveto members. The reason can be found by considering the basic model that gave this result: a nonveto vote makes a difference only if all five veto members plus exactly three other nonveto members support the resolution. (If more than three support it, that member's vote becomes redundant, if less than three, its vote is ineffective.) Given the many ways states can line up for and against a resolution, this configuration is a relatively unlikely event. It is rare that a nonveto player will be in a position to make a difference. Thus, if the assumptions made here about voting are correct (and this is an important condition), states should not be striving to join the Council in quest of the vote per se. Their demands should be justified on some other basis. We will modify these voting assumptions later by adding alliances, but even then it will remain true that a member without a veto has almost no power.

A second result worth noting comes from comparing the current Council with the one generated by adding a nonveto member (comparing the second and third rows). The power of each nonveto member falls as one more joins. This is not surprising since each one must share the power with more of the others. The *degree* to which the nonveto members' powers falls, however, is surprising. The *total* power of all the nonveto members taken together falls, even though there are more of them. It goes from a total power of 0.0186 with 10 nonveto members to 0.0141 with 11. The common-sense expectation would be that adding

TABLE 4.1
Degrees of Power for Various Types of Security Councils, Without Alliances

RULES:	Each Veto Member's Power	Each Nonveto Member's Power	Total Power Veto	Total Power Nonveto
ORIGINAL: 11 members 5 veto, 6 non 7 = majority	0.197	0.00216	0.987	0.0130
CURRENT: 15 members 5 veto, 10 non 9 = majority	0.196	0.00186	0.981	0.0186
ADD A NONVETO MEMBER: 16 members 5 veto, 11 non 9 = majority	0.197	0.00128	0.985	0.0141
INCREASE NONVETO MEMBERS AND MAJORITY QUOTA: 16 members 5 veto, 11 non 10 = majority	0.192	0.00420	0.958	0.0420
ADD A VETO MEMBER: 16 members 6 veto, 10 non 9 = majority	0.166	0.00034	0.996	0.0034

more nonveto members would increase their power vis-à-vis the Big Five, but the Shapley-Shubik analysis claims it is not so.

Who is right, Shapley and Shubik or common sense? Is there some reason why adding more members and votes hurts the power of the whole nonveto group, or should we conclude that the Shapley-Shubik index is flawed? I believe the index is right, and it is possible to construct an explanation why. If the Big Five favor some resolution, they currently need four more votes to pass it. They must dip into the pool of the other ten states to come up with four votes. With eleven small states instead of ten, the Big Five have a bigger pool and may have a better prospect of finding those four extra votes.

In February 1995, the Non-Aligned Movement (NAM) called for enlarging the Security Council to 26. Some of the new members might be permanent, according to the NAM, but even keeping permanent membership to the current 5, the Council should be expanded, it said. Italy's UN ambassador, Francesco Paolo Fulci, argued recently for a similar change of including 20 nonpermanent members with no new veto members. The present analysis suggests that this kind of change would make essentially no difference in terms of voting power. The voting power of a nonveto member is already minuscule and adding more members might reduce it even further. A nonveto seat on the Security Council might confer prestige, information, and involvement with decisions, but it is not something to seek for pure voting power.

A third result of the analysis is that the decline in power with new members can be offset by increasing the required majority, or "action threshold" in UN parlance. In the fourth row of the table, the majority required is raised from 9 votes to 10, and the result is a large relative increase in the small members' powers. The Big Five would find it harder to get 5 extra votes than 4. (The extreme case would increase the Council majority requirement to 15; then all members would in effect have a veto.) The question of what the action threshold should be has received less attention than the numbers of states that should be on the Council, but this analysis suggests it is relevant to the relative voting power.

The principle illustrated is that adding nonpermanent members decreases the total power of the nonveto group, while raising the majority requirement increases it. The trade-off between majority requirement and nonpermanent membership is shown in Table 4.2, for a 26-member Council as envisaged by the NAM, with 5 veto members. The present rule of thumb of setting the majority between ½ and ⅔ would suggest a majority of 14, 15, 16, or 17. A majority rule of 14 turns out to be just enough to restore the total power of the nonpermanent members (i.e., to bring it back to its current level of 0.0186).

Does this mean that small states would be wise to push for a higher action threshold? *Absolute* voting power conveyed by membership is tiny for any reasonable majority quota. Voting power

TABLE 4.2
Total Power of Nonveto Members as a Function of the Number of Nonveto Members

26 MEMBER COUNCIL
5 VETO MEMBERS

Majority required	Total power of nonveto members
13	0.0120
14	0.0196
15	0.0304
16	0.0457
17	0.0664
18	0.0941

considerations may be slight compared to such issues as prestige and access to information. A higher threshold could make the Council unwieldy and might prompt resistance from states concerned with an effective United Nations.

Satisfaction versus Power

A tale from the American South tells of a mother and father who are worrying about their little son. He is four years old but has never said a word. Years pass, all his playmates have learned to talk, the parents wait and hope, but he has still never spoken. On the morning of his seventh birthday, he sits down to breakfast, and tells his mother, "These pancakes need more salt!" His parents are amazed and delighted, and ask him why he has never spoken all these years. "Well, until now," he says, "everything has been going along just fine."

Satisfaction and power are different.[8] A state may feel that the Security Council's decisions have been "going along just fine," even though it has had no influence on them. The state's allies on the Council may be taking care of its business. Conversely, a state can be a full-fledged permanent member but feel frustrated if Council actions are continually blocked by others' vetoes. We can examine satisfaction within the basic voting model by calculating a slightly different proba-

TABLE 4.3
Six Possible Outcomes Concerning a Resolution, Contributing to Satisfaction, Power, or Neither

	I support the resolution	I oppose the resolution
Passes with me & passes without me	Satisfaction	—
Passes with me & fails without me	Satisfaction & Power	Satisfaction & Power
Fails with me & fails without me	—	Satisfaction

bility than before. My power was defined as the *probability that the Council would have changed its vote, given I had changed my vote*. My satisfaction is the *probability that the Council would pass a resolution I want passed, or reject a resolution I want rejected*.

The relationship between satisfaction and power is shown in Table 4.3. The table includes various possibilities: I can support or oppose the resolution, and the resolution can pass with me or without me, with me but not without me, or fail with me or without me. This generates six possible situations that I might face. Some of these outcomes contribute to my satisfaction and power, some to my satisfaction alone, and some to neither, as indicated in Table 4.3.

The degrees of a member's satisfaction in various versions of the Security Council are shown in Table 4.4.

The numbers can be compared with an imaginary situation where there is no Security Council to take actions on problems that arise, nor any other way of doing the Council's job, so that each issue has an outcome that is unrelated to the states' desires. This is an extreme assumption, introduced only to help us understand the meaning of the figures. Each of the two outcomes would then be equally likely according to the basic model, would occur independent of the states' desires, and the expected satisfaction would be exactly 0.5, as shown in the first row. Setting up a Council under current rules increases the satisfaction to 0.61903 for those not on it. Their satisfaction is raised because,

TABLE 4.4
Degrees of Satisfaction for Various Kinds of Security Councils, without Alliances

Rules	Satisf'n of nonmember	Satisf'n of nonveto member	Satisf'n of veto member	Average satisf'n	Probability of passing resolution
NO COUNCIL	0.5	—	—	0.5	—
ORIGINAL: 11 members 5 veto, 6 non 7 = majority	0.61898	0.61995	0.6654	0.624	0.1654
CURRENT: 15 members 5 veto, 10 non 9 = majority	0.61903	0.61990	0.6650	0.620	0.1649
ENLARGED: 23 members 7 veto, 16 non 14 = majority	0.59719	0.59739	0.6245	0.600	0.1245
ENLARGED: 23 members 10 veto, 13 non 14 = majority	0.57576	0.575765	0.5909	0.578	0.0909

according to the basic model of voting, some resolutions are popular and others unpopular, so states have common interests, and even those without a vote can expect the Council members to reflect their views to some degree. Having a vote but no veto raises satisfaction a little, up to 0.61990, less than 1 percent beyond nonmembership. Having a veto raises it significantly, to 0.6650, 38 percent beyond nonmembership (based on a minimum value of 0.5). The maximum would be to seize control of the Council as dictator where one would always get one's way. Satisfaction would go to 1.

The table gives two possible future Councils, one with two veto members, perhaps Germany and Japan, and another with three more, perhaps Brazil, India, and Nigeria. The effect of adding veto members is to decrease overall satisfaction. Resolutions that most members want passed do not get passed—some state or another vetoes them. This is shown in the last column of the table, where the proportion of resolutions passed drops sharply. In fact, comparing the current Council with the final 10-veto arrangement, a state would be more satisfied as a nonmember in the current setup (0.61903) than as a full-fledged veto member in the enlarged Council (0.59090). What it gains by promoting or blocking particular resolutions it dislikes is more than lost by other individual members blocking measures it likes.

The fourth column shows the average satisfaction calculated over the entire United Nations membership. For example, for the value for the year 1945, we have 5 veto members, 6 nonveto members and 40 nonmembers of the Security Council. The weighted average of satisfaction is 0.624. As the United Nations grows and as the Security Council adds more veto members, satisfaction slips back toward 0.5, the value associated with no Council at all. The Security Council is hampered by too many vetoes. (When we add the consideration of naturally occurring alliances, this situation will be found to be less serious.)

Deliberate Continuing Alliances

An example in the introduction showed how a continuing alliance can increase the allies' total powers. Alliances are usually helpful to power, though not always—it sometimes pays voters to stay separate, according to the Shapley-Shubik index.[9] The simplest way to generate a continuing alliance is to make an agreement to vote together, one that all members can trust. The coalition decides internally how it will vote, some members suppressing their true desires regarding the issue before them right now in exchange for solidarity and long-term influence. Such was the case with the non-aligned movement of the 1950s, and another kind of bloc over many years included the Soviet Union, Belarus, and the Ukraine, whose three votes were always cast alike since they really came from one country. Some results are shown in the table below. Here a group of nonveto members have made the agreement to stay together, and we have calculated the average power of each single state in the group.

TABLE 4.5
Power as a Function of a Bloc of Nonveto Members

CURRENT COUNCIL,
WITH A BLOC AMONG SOME NONVETO MEMBERS

Size of Bloc	Power of Bloc Member
1	0.0019
2	0.0021
3	0.0027
4	0.0038
5	0.0061
6	0.0111
7	0.0238
8	0.0208
9	0.0185
10	0.0167

Table 4.5 shows an understandable pattern. There is an incentive to band together up to a bloc of size seven. Only three nonveto members are outside of it at that point, and the three are not enough to help the Big Five pass a resolution. The alliance has become a full player with a "sixth veto." Adding allies beyond seven gives no further power to the bloc, but increases the number who want a share of the power gained, so the average power goes down. From the viewpoint of the bloc members, seven is the ideal number.[10]

While forming a coalition seems like a good tactic, two caveats should be noted. One is that we have ignored countercoalitions. There is nothing to prevent other members responding to one's bloc by forming their own bloc, in which case the numbers in Table 4.5 would fall. Another problem is the credibility of the members' commitments to vote together. Could they really trust each other to resist the bribes and threats of the five powerful states who want them to desert? Part of the reason there has been so little deliberate bloc formation among the non-aligned states is that the blocs would be unlikely to stick together.

Natural Continuing Alliances

The Shapley-Shubik index was designed to be politically naive. It was meant to measure the power of a state based solely on a constitution, behind the proverbial veil of ignorance, without knowing the details of personalities or politics. This is appropriate for an index that measures the properties of a constitutional scheme, but relies too much on assuming that all voting patterns are equally likely. For a given p (the "popularity" of a resolution, the probability that a state will vote for it) each country's vote is probabilistically independent of the others, in the sense that learning one country's vote should not influence our expectation at all of how another will vote. This is proper for a definition of abstract voting power, but as a description of a particular body it is quite implausible. Continuing patterns of mutual support abound in the United Nations, even without commitments to vote together. Knowing the United Kingdom's vote tells us something about Canada's, not with certainty but with high probability. However, several subsequent analyses have generalized the index to cases where there is an expectation of likely alliances.[11] We will alter the model to describe how continuing alliances might function. The way we will do it is to devise a general framework, then fit it to the data of recent voting patterns in the UN.

One possibility is to use the notion just described, to assume that countries divide into groups, each with perfect discipline so that members within a bloc vote alike. This is admirably simple, but unrealistic. Instead we will choose a representation that gives countries more flexibility and that seems to fit the data better. It is a spatial model and allows strict blocs but also looser configurations in which states tend to vote alike but can sometimes differ.[12] Each member of the voting body is assigned a point in a space. The member's point is an *ideal point*, representing the position that the member would most like the body to adopt. In many countries one can define a liberal-conservative continuum and place legislators on it, but in our case the states lie in a two-dimensional plane. (This choice is based partly on the data and partly on practical judgment—adding a second dimension seemed necessary to portray the pattern of voting; going to three dimensions would fit somewhat better but would be harder to interpret.) A resolution is represented by two points in the plane, an "adopt" point and a "reject" point. To decide how to vote, a state judges which point is closer to its ideal. If the adopt point is closer than reject, the member votes yes, but if the reject point is closer, the member votes no. A continuing alliance among some members is represented by putting them close together in the space. If they are near to each other they will vote alike on the various resolutions that arise because they want almost the same thing.

How do we know where to place the voters' ideal points and the resolutions' adopt and reject points? As academic analysts our problem is the reverse of the voters' decision. They know where their ideal point is and they must calculate distances to decide how to vote. We know how they voted and want to construct a spatial configuration that fits their votes. One approximate solution to our problem is to use the principle that states voting alike are nearby in the hypothetical space, so we will try to place states at points whose proximities reflect correlations in their voting patterns. Computer algorithms for multidimensional scaling do just this, assigning countries with higher correlation coefficients between their patterns of voting to points that are nearby in space.

Although the Security Council has been making decisions at a high rate, much of its deliberation is secret, conducted without formal votes. The votes actually recorded consist mainly of Yes votes, with No and Abstain relatively rare. They do not seem to be indicators of positions or powers now, and certainly not of those in a divisive crisis that might arise. Many of the Council's current actions are now taken without votes at all, and a plausible view is that a state's formal power influences the outcome of negotiations that are never in the end put to a vote. For these reasons, and for the purpose of acquiring an adequate amount of data, the scaling analysis was based not on votes from the Security Council but from the General Assembly. The working assumption was that the votes of Council members in the General Assembly indicated how close those countries' interests are in general. Clearly there are problems with taking any vote as indicating the voter's true position, because of tendencies to make plans behind the scenes, bend to the influence of others, and avoid bringing issues to a vote that one knows will fail. But if we do not read too much into the results, if we do not try to assign importance to exact numbers but come to conclusions only from their general pattern, the assumption should not mislead us.

I analyze the same set of votes from the 46th, 47th, and 48th sessions used by Kim and Russett. Kim and Russett calculated correlation coefficients as measures of voting similarity among states. The multidimensional scaling routine used for this chapter tried to duplicate only the order of correlations, rather than trying to match proximity with magnitude of the correlation.

The analysis was conducted for a set of 23 states determined by the 1995 Security Council augmented by some reasonable members, balanced for regions. In this enlarged Council with 23 members,

Power and Satisfaction in the Security Council 73

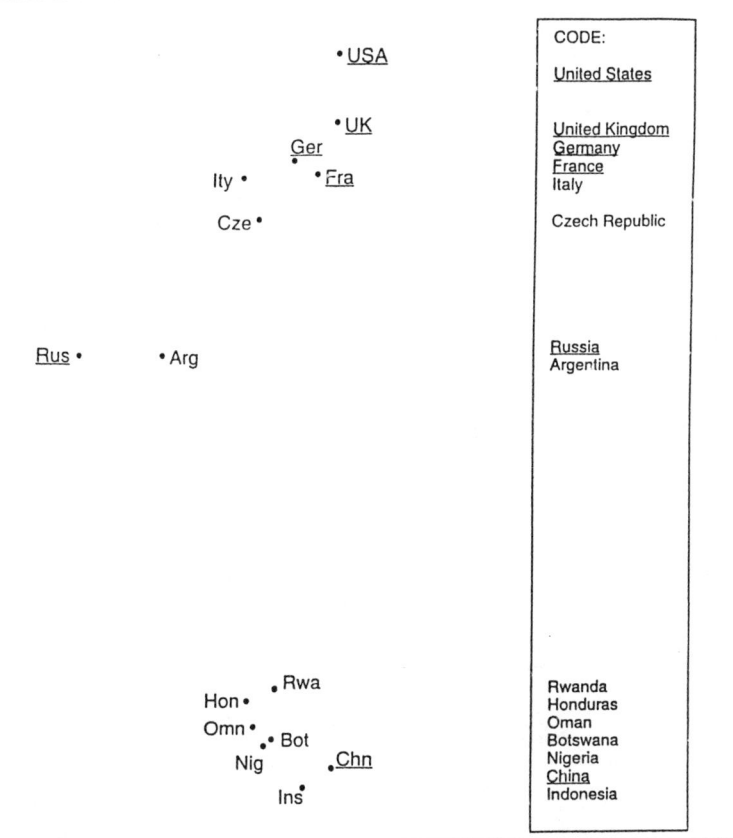

FIGURE 4.1: Positions in Ideological Space of the 1995 15-Member Security Council

Germany and Japan have vetoes. The results of multidimensional scaling are shown in Figures 4.1 and 4.2. Figure 4.1 shows the positions of a subset of the total 23, the actual 1995 Security Council, while Figure 4.2 shows the entire 23. The figures illustrate both the structure of the current international system and the logic of multidimensional scaling. The most obvious feature is the prominence of a North-South dimension. The United States is at one end, followed by the Western European states. (The rules for excluding votes, which dropped resolutions that were near unanimous, probably led to an understatement of U.S.

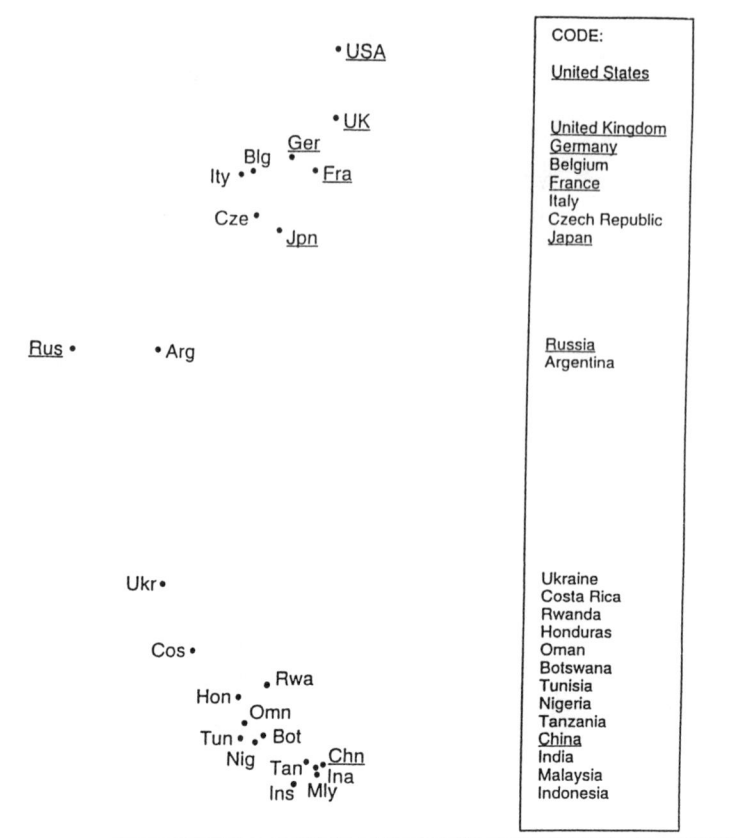

FIGURE 4.2: Positions in Ideological Space of a Hypothetical 23-Member Security Council

isolation.) At the other end are China, Indonesia, and other states from Africa, Asia, and Central America. The orientation of the figure can be chosen arbitrarily, so we have chosen this dimension as vertical. The figure shows that most of a country's voting behavior can be predicted by where it lies on this one dimension. The pattern is generally similar to that found by Kim and Russett, even though their study used the different technique of factor analysis to scale the similarities of states.

Another influence seems to enter voting choices. Both France and Russia are between the extremes of the North-South dimension.

They voted differently from each other, however, often disagreeing on Middle East issues and questions of intervention. Accordingly the computer scaling routine added a second dimension, and this new direction allowed them to be separated from each other.

As before, voting power is the probability that one's vote would make a difference and satisfaction is the probability that one is on the winning side. To calculate voting power and satisfaction we need an account of what resolutions are likely to come before the body. If a resolution is represented by two points, an accept and a reject point, a natural plan is to place those points on the space at random. Here we drew a circle and dropped the two points randomly within it, uniformly over its area.[13] The center of the circle was the midpoint of the two extreme states on each dimension, and the radius was set so that about the same number of motions passed in this model of the current Council, one in six, as passed in the last section's model without alliances. This is of course a much lower proportion than passes in the real Council, but it seems likely that many ideas do not become formal resolutions because it is recognized beforehand that they would fail.

Abstentions were introduced by assigning a fixed probability that a country did not vote on a given resolution. This probability was 5 percent, independent of the country's position on the resolution and of any other votes cast. Countries had to abstain on these resolutions and they received no power from them.[14] The effect of adding abstentions was very small—on rare occasions it allowed the nonpermanent members to make a difference, especially those that were near only one veto member. The powers are too hard to calculate exactly, so they were estimated using Monte Carlo simulation. With one million imaginary votes cast in each computer simulation, the results should be accurate, especially for the larger powers of the veto countries. The results are shown in Table 4.6.[15]

Again nonveto members have insignificant power. In a more realistic model, their powers would be near zero. China is by far the most powerful member, about twice as powerful as other veto members. This is due to China's political position reflected in votes taken so far—it stands alone with a veto at an extreme position. This means it is constantly using its veto or threat to veto (actually or only implicitly), and so it is constantly making a difference. The United States is also at an extreme point, but it is less powerful than China because other Western veto members are nearby, and often

TABLE 4.6
Power and Satisfaction in an Enlarged Security Council, with Natural Alliances.
(Veto members are underlined)

	CURRENT			ENLARGED		
	country	power	satisf'n	country	power	satisf'n
Africa	Botswana	0	0.655	Botswana	0	0.655
—	Nigeria	0	0.653	Nigeria	0	0.653
—	Oman	0	0.654	Oman	0	0.654
—	Rwanda	0	0.659	Rwanda	0	0.659
—	—	—	0.651	Tunisia	0	0.651
—	—	—	0.658	Tanzania	0	0.658
Asia	<u>China</u>	<u>0.334</u>	<u>0.660</u>	<u>China</u>	<u>0.254</u>	<u>0.660</u>
—	Indonesia	0	0.648	Indonesia	0	0.648
—	—	—	0.657	India	0	0.657
—	—	—	0.660	<u>Japan</u>	<u>0.118</u>	<u>0.660</u>
—	—	—	0.657	Malaysia	0	0.657
East	Czech	0.0004	0.660	Czech	0.0002	0.659
Europe	<u>Russia</u>	<u>0.189</u>	<u>0.660</u>	<u>Russia</u>	<u>0.145</u>	<u>0.660</u>
—	—	—	0.656	Ukraine	0	0.656
Latin	Argentina	0.0004	0.659	Argentina	0.0002	0.659
America	Honduras	0	0.656	Honduras	0	0.656
—	—	—	0.651	Costa Rica	0	0.651
West	<u>France</u>	<u>0.155</u>	<u>0.659</u>	<u>France</u>	<u>0.118</u>	<u>0.659</u>
Europe	Germany	0.0004	0.660	Germany	0.118	0.660
& other	<u>USA</u>	<u>0.165</u>	<u>0.659</u>	<u>USA</u>	<u>0.126</u>	<u>0.659</u>
—	<u>UK</u>	<u>0.155</u>	<u>0.660</u>	<u>UK</u>	<u>0.118</u>	<u>0.660</u>
—	Italy	0.0004	0.660	Italy	0	0.660
—	—	—	0.660	Belgium	0.0002	0.660

join it to defeat a resolution. If the resolution was doomed even if the United States had not been there, it does not get credit for the rejection.

This is a basic result: that veto countries that are extreme and isolated from other veto countries enjoy high power. If the voting procedure changed to majority rule, then countries in the center of the diagram would hold the balance—they would be pivotal to the success of a resolution and be assigned higher power than the extremes. Just why an extreme veto player is so powerful can be understood by Figure 4.3. States A and B are close together in ideological space while C is more distant. A point inside the dotted triangle is Pareto-optimal, meaning that any shift from it will displease one or more of the players. If the

Power and Satisfaction in the Security Council 77

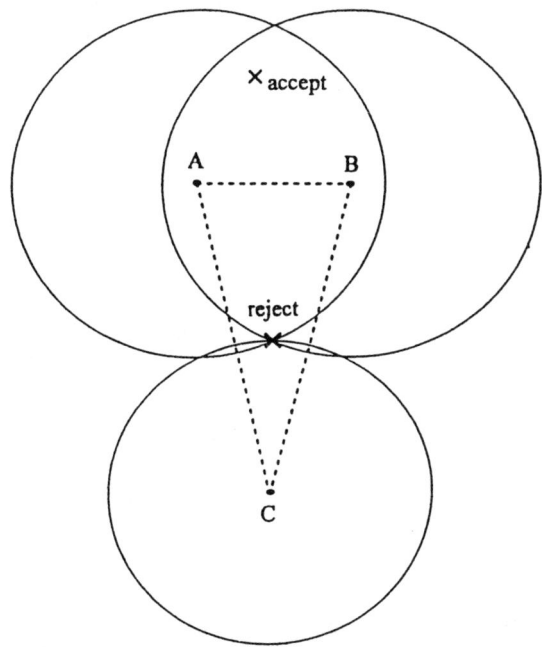

FIGURE 4.3: An Illustration of Veto Voting in a 3-Member Council

"reject" outcome is in that triangle, as is the one shown, no other motion can defeat it since all three states have vetoes. We draw three circles throughout the reject outcome centered on the ideal points of the three states. All points inside A's circle are preferred to "reject," and all points inside B's circle are likewise preferred. Thus if C were not there, an "accept" outcome at any point inside the large lens-shaped area representing the intersection of these two sets would be selected over "reject." C will veto such a motion, however, and in doing so will be making a difference to the outcome and manifesting its power. The corresponding areas where A or B's presence would make a difference for that reject motion are the two small intersections. Since the likelihood of an "accept" outcome ending up in one of the three lenses is proportional to their areas, C holds much more power for this situation. This is only one case—this argument depends on a certain position of the "reject"—but for other placements the result is more complicated but similar. The proximity of A and B gives them a large area of overlapping interest. They are ready to accomplish a lot together, and C's power consists in frustrating their plans.

These considerations raise the question of whether power is the appropriate goal. If the United States stops a resolution it does not want, does it care whether it was the *sole* cause of the rejection? In the 23-member Council it would be somewhat less satisfied than China, but the discrepancy is far less than one might expect by the difference in their powers. Of course, China would be more able to extract side payments to alter its vote, since someone trying to induce the Western bloc of veto members would have to divide up the payment among several countries. But in terms of the present simple model of voting where a country votes for what it wants, power and satisfaction are quite different. Satisfaction for the current Council is quite high among some countries who are not members, such as Japan. The least satisfied country on the Council is Indonesia, at an extreme point in the space without the protection of a veto.

One notable fact is the overall similarity of the smaller and larger Security Councils. The pattern of powers is the same, although in the larger Council it is more diffused among the new veto states. The profile of satisfactions is the same. Unlike a model of the Security Council with no natural alliance pattern, here adding members can mean duplicating the behavior of nearby ones already there. New veto members do not increase the blockage because the rejected resolutions would usually not have passed anyway.

To a degree these results may be artifacts of the method of analysis, using a three-year slice to estimate where the countries stand. Even though 131 resolutions were included, the number of different issues they comprise is much smaller, and future sessions may bring up differences that divide the countries quite differently. The configuration of states shown may be unstable. How will it look in the diagrams drawn after 5 or 25 years? Since no one can be sure, the states may see a veto as an insurance policy. Current alliances may be temporary, so they want a veto to protect their interests. If this is an attraction of veto, that reason should be explicitly recognized in the debate on Council reform, since there may be alternative ways to achieve the same end.

Conclusions

Some of the conclusions of the analysis are these:

- A veto gives a state high voting power, no veto means a state has almost none; to a fair approximation as far as voting is concerned, the Security Council has five members.
- Granting more seats to the nonveto players can diminish their total power; however, their absolute power is so small, before and after, that the change makes little real difference.
- Power more accurately depends not only on the voting rules, but on who a state can expect to support or oppose it.
- Gaining a vote gives you less power if other powerful countries are already voting the way you would.
- Standing at an extreme political position, isolated from other veto states, gives a veto state high power.
- Adding new veto members hinders the body from acting, but this effect is small if the new members stand near positions already occupied by current veto members.
- Power is not the most sensible goal in this context; it can constitute a form of insurance against future surprises, but states should also seek satisfaction with the Council's votes, which may not require them to hold formal voting rights.

In some ways the history of reform seems like an ironic joke, a trap set by a malevolent deity hoping to draw the organization into conflict. The trickster laid the plans in 1945, inducing the victors of World War II to assign themselves veto power, rationalized by the expectation that they would bear the burden of the UN's work. Many delegates at the founding 50 years ago objected to the rules and over the years the pressure for reform has increased, while the problem becomes more difficult to solve. The 1945 Charter identified three nations as former "enemy states," but by 1995 two of these "enemy states" had become two of the three biggest financial contributors. The 1945 Charter set out no easy way to change representation as the world changed. Now 135 more states have joined, and the proportion of states represented in the Council has shrunk from 22 percent to 8 percent. European-oriented states are greatly overrepresented there, and whole areas are greatly underrepresented. The end of the Cold War increased the power of the United Nations as a whole and the power of the Security Council within it, so excluded states became more eager to participate. At the same time it increased the number of European states competing for a place, and bolstered the claim of Germany in particular. None of the veto states, upon whose unanimous approval a Charter change depends, seems motivated to give up its status. Demands for a change have increased, but it is not clear how one could be agreed on.

These conclusions point to a general thesis: many proposed changes in voting rules really do not matter. Changes in real voting power seem politically difficult to achieve. Security Council membership is important for other reasons, so if these other reasons are explicitly recognized in the debate, the problem will become easier to solve.

NOTES

1. Lloyd Shapley and Martin Shubik, "A Method for Evaluating the Distribution of Power in a Committee System," *American Political Science Review* 58 (1954), pp. 787-92.
2. Robert Dahl, "The Concept of Power," *Behavioral Science* 2 (1957), pp. 201-15.
3. Philip Straffin, "The Shapley-Shubik and Banzhaf Power Indices as Probabilities," in A. Roth, ed., *The Shapley Value* (Cambridge: Cambridge University Press, 1988), pp. 72-82.
4. Traditionally the Shapley-Shubik index has been justified by ranking the members in order of their enthusiasm for the motion and assigning the power for that ranking to the pivotal person, the one who puts the motion over the top. Someone's power is then the probability of being pivotal for a randomly chosen ranking. This is often an efficient way to calculate power, but Straffin's approach seems more convincing as a rationale.
5. For example, John Banzhaf, "Weighted Voting Doesn't Work: A Mathematical Analysis," *Rutgers Law Review* 18 (1965), pp. 317-43; J. Deagan and E. Packel, "A New Index of Power for Simple Person Games," *International Journal of Game Theory* 7 (1979), pp. 113-23; P. Dubey and Lloyd Shapley, "Mathematical Properties of the Banzhaf Index," *Mathematics of Operations Research* 4 (1979), pp. 99-131; Tatsuaki Kuroda, "A Power Index for Multistage and Multiagent Decision Systems," *Behavioral Science* 37 (1993), pp. 255-73.
6. In 1954, when they first explained their measure, Shapley and Shubik illustrated it with the Security Council, and such studies have appeared intermittently since. Also see William Dixon, "The Evaluation of Weighted Voting Schemes for the United Nations General Assembly," *International Studies Quarterly* 27 (1983), pp. 295-314. Noting that under the 1950 Uniting for Peace Resolution the General Assembly is entitled to act on peacekeeping when the Security

Council is blocked, Gerhard Schwodiauer, "Calculation of A Priori Power Distributions for the United Nations," *Research Memorandum* 24 (Vienna: Institut für Höhere Studien, 1968), included the idea that under the 1950 Uniting for Peace Resolution *any* nine members of the Security Council can call for an emergency session of the General Assembly to consider a matter of peace and security that has been blocked in the Council. This resolution gives the nonpermanent members an extra element of power, but the situation is complex since the General Assembly's ability to enforce its decisions is far less than the Security Council's. The resolution was used in the 1956 Suez crisis, as well as regarding United States actions in Granada and Panama. The calculations in this chapter do not take account of it, so one should recognize it as a limited qualification to some of the conclusions about the lower power of the nonpermanent members. Steven Brams, *Game Theory and Politics* (New York: Free Press, 1975), compared the Shapley-Shubik index with the Banzhaf measure of power and looked at likelihoods of motions passing or being blocked. Francese Carreras and Antonio Magana, "The Multilinear Extension and the Modified Banzhaf-Coleman Index," *Mathematical Social Sciences* 28 (1994), pp. 215-22, used the Security Council as a way to illustrate their method of calculation. William Kerby and Frank Goebler, "The Distribution of Voting Power in the UN: A Power Index Analysis of Some Proposals for a Reform of the UN Security Council," *Mathematisches Seminar der Universität Hamburg* (Germany: June 1995 mimeo), calculated the power of all countries in the United Nations on the prospect that they might some day be on the Security Council, considering that certain quotas of nonpermanent seats are allotted to different regions. They also looked at changes in the veto rule, such as a requirement that at least *two* permanent members vote against a resolution to reject it. I have not pursued it here because it is unlikely to be acceptable (see chapter eight).

7. For example, Lloyd Shapley, *A Comparison of Power Indices and a Nonsymmetric Generalization* (Santa Monica, Cal.: Rand Corporation, 1971).
8. Steven Brams and M. Lake, "Power and Satisfaction in a Representative Democracy," in P. Ordeshook, ed., *Game Theory and Political Science* (New York: New York University Press, 1978), pp. 529-62; Philip Straffin, Morton Davis, and Steven Brams, "Power and Satisfaction in an Ideologically Divided Voting Body," in M. Holler, ed., *Power, Voting, and Voting Power* (Wurzburg: Physica-Verlag, 1981), pp. 239-55.
9. Christopher Nevison, "Structural Power and Satisfaction in Simple Games," in S. Brams, A. Schotter, and G. Schwodiauer, eds., *Applied Game Theory* (Wurzburg: Physica-Verlag, 1979), pp. 39-57.
10. Some calculations on cohesive subgroups in the spirit of the Banzhav index are given by P. Fishburn and W. Gehrlein, "Power of Subgroups in Voting Bodies," *Social Choice and Welfare* 1 (1984), pp. 85-95.
11. G. Owen, "Political Games," *Naval Research Logistics Quarterly* 18 (1971), pp. 345-55; Lloyd Shapley, "A Comparison of Power Indices and Nonsymmetric Generalization," Rand Corporation Paper P-5872 (Santa Monica, Cal: Rand Corporation, 1977); G. Owen and Lloyd Shapley, "Optimal Location of

Candidates in Ideological Space," *International Journal of Game Theory* 18 (1989), pp. 339-56.

12. This method was proposed as a model for the United States Congress by Duncan MacRae in *Dimensions of Congressional Voting* (Berkeley: University of California Press, 1958), and in more recent sophisticated forms by Keith Poole and Howard Rosenthal in "Ideology, Party, and Voting in the U.S. Congress," *American Political Science Review* 79 (1985), pp. 373-99; it has been applied to study every Congressional session since 1790. See Keith Poole and Howard Rosenthal, "Patterns of Congressional Voting," *American Journal of Political Science* 35 (1991), pp. 228-78.

13. Note that I do not put "reject" points systematically closer to the member's positions. One might argue for doing this, on the grounds that past Council actions have brought the status quo closer to where the general opinion wants it. The alternative I used reflects a more turbulent, less controllable world.

14. The abstention rate in Security Council votes for these years was only about 2 percent. As explained above I do not wish to use votes actually taken as indicators of the operation of the rules, so the 5 percent rate should be regarded as arbitrary, but if anything exaggerating the effect of abstentions. The conclusions seem quite sturdy for different abstention rates. According to Article 27(3), a state, even a veto member, must abstain if the matter is one of peace and security in which it has a direct interest. Members have been reluctant to enforce this when it matters, against the veto members involved in the crisis. France and Britain, for example, did not abstain during the 1956 Suez crisis. (See N. White, *The United Nations and the Maintenance of International Peace and Security* [Manchester: Manchester University Press, 1990].) Actual absences are very rare, though one (the Soviet Union during consideration of measures at the beginning of the Korean War in 1950) made a big difference.

15. In the no alliance case the members' powers, defined as their likelihoods of making a difference, always sum to 1. Here this is no longer true, and I have normalized them to sum to 1.

5

CHINA'S VOTING PATTERN IN THE SECURITY COUNCIL, 1990–1995

NIGEL THALAKADA

Most observers recognize a new-found concert among four of the great powers—permanent members of the Security Council—since the political reorientation of the Soviet Union. Yet the role of another country, the People's Republic of China, whose views are equally important in the Council, goes relatively unexamined. Beijing has demonstrated an increasing independence in the formulation of its foreign policy, from being an ally of the Soviet Union before the Sino-Soviet split to sharing strategic interests with the United States during the 1970s, to treating the U.S. with wariness in the late 1980s and 1990s. In short, while the Soviet Union, and then Russia, could increasingly be relied upon to cooperate with the United States and its Western allies in the maintenance of international security, China has exercised considerable geopolitical influence by vacillating between collaboration and aloofness. This behavior is especially evident in the pattern of China's voting in the Security Council, where it abstained on more than 20 occasions in the period 1990–1995. In this chapter I elucidate the reasons for this behavior by examining accounts of Chinese foreign policy objectives in the post–Cold War era and assessing the results of its votes in the Security Council, both in terms of its foreign policy objectives and rewards (tangible and intangible) gained, most especially from the U.S.

Under Article 27, paragraph 3, of the UN Charter, the affirmative vote of all 5 permanent members of the Security Council—China, France, the Soviet Union, the United Kingdom, and the United States (identified in Article 23, paragraph 1)—is required (along with the concurring votes of at least 4 nonpermanent members in a Council of 15) for the passage of a resolution on nonprocedural matters. In practice, however, the absence or abstention of a permanent member is not counted as a negative vote. Between 1946 and 1990, the veto was exercised 279 times, 124 by the Soviet Union, 82 by the U.S., 33 by the U.K., 22 by China (1 of which by the Republic of China [Taiwan], which occupied China's seat in the UN until 25 October 1971), and 18 by France.[1] Since 1991, the veto has been cast only three times—twice by the Soviet Union/Russia and once by the United States. While this development suggests the existence of great power comity on matters of serious international concern, the threat of the veto's use has not disappeared altogether. Whereas the Soviet Union most often threatened the veto (and carried through with it) during the Cold War, China has since become the power to use the veto threat most frequently. Yet, as we shall see, there are competing goals in Chinese foreign policy. To achieve a compromise in cases in which they possess conflicting interests, the Chinese have abstained in Security Council votes. Often, the trade-off involves a balancing of principle and prudence.

The Competing Objectives of Chinese Foreign Policy

Akin to the dialectic of its official Marxist-Leninist ideology, Chinese foreign policy under Deng Xiaoping navigates a tortuous route between the dictates of official ideology and the material benefits of pragmatism. After the Sino-Soviet split, China remained isolated from much of the world. In the early 1970s, once the Manichean view of Mao's early "two-world" model gave way to the "three-world" model (which could accommodate the notion of the nonaligned or third camp, between the imperial and socialist worlds), Chinese foreign policy pronouncements increasingly proclaimed solidarity with the Third World, which became a symbol for China's struggle against imperialist exploitation and the persistent underdevelopment of the countries of the South. Such solidarity might be better seen as an attempt by Beijing to enhance its international geopolitical role more than actually to represent developing countries' interests, as revealed by Beijing's unwillingness to prevent the genocide in Bosnia-Herzegovina in spite of widespread support among developing countries for stronger measures to prevent Serb aggression against Bosnian Muslims.[2]

After Mao's death and the ascension of Deng to the leadership of the Chinese Communist Party (CCP), China's foreign policy became more materialist in orientation, reflecting a desire by the CCP to shore up whatever domestic legitimacy it had after the debacles of the Great Leap Forward (1957-1959) and the Cultural Revolution (1966-1976) by promoting internal economic development. International organizations, such as the World Bank, became instruments in the service of Chinese national interests by providing a source of information, knowledge, capital, and technology without a concomitant loss of political autonomy.[3] Yet just as there were internal and external systemic incentives to pursue a moderate course of partial involvement in the emerging global economic interdependence, China remained wedded to the principle of absolute state sovereignty as reflecting its national interest and for cultural and historical reasons.

China's historical experience of Western and Japanese imperialism during a "century of national humiliation" strongly imbued Chinese thinking with Westphalian notions of absolute state sovereignty and the salience of power politics in international politics. This line of thought became all the more pronounced after the international censure of China in the wake of the Tiananmen Square massacre on 4 June 1989. The events of that day and the international outrage over it were poignant reminders of the growing chasm between the conception of popular sovereignty embraced by the West and the Chinese conception of state sovereignty. For the Chinese political leadership, because there could not possibly exist such a thing as human rights without the community and state authority, the principle of state sovereignty is prior to, and always superior to, the principle of human rights.[4] As seen by China, attempts by the West to impose its conception of human rights constituted nothing less than a threat to the sovereignty of the Chinese state. Not much less of a threat to the CCP's authority is the logic of global economic interdependence, which Western leaders explicitly hope will lead to the peaceful evolution of China into a liberal polity. The foremost statement of China's principled position on the sanctity of state sovereignty is Deng's Five Principles of Peaceful Co-existence: mutual respect for sovereignty and territorial integrity, mutual nonaggression, mutual noninterference in internal affairs, equality and mutual benefit, and peaceful co-existence.

Hence, Chinese foreign policy should be understood to promote the national interest in two ways: first, by encouraging internal economic development in order to preserve the CCP's domestic legitimacy and enhance China's international prestige; and second, by protecting the political autonomy of the state. Yet, as might be expected, these goals are often incompatible; therein lies the challenge for Chinese leaders to formulate a policy that best serves the national interest and for the disinterested observer to comprehend the motivations behind Chinese foreign policy behavior.

China's strategy has been described by Samuel Kim as "maxi-mini," i.e., maximizing security or economic benefits while minimizing responsibilities. This characterization is manifest in China's attitude towards the Security Council. Although China treats the Council as an important forum for the exposition of its views and the exercise of its great power status, China demonstrates little concern for the Council's principal raison d'etre, the maintenance of international order.[5] China has not actually cast a veto since 1989, when it stopped a move by Western countries to support the anticommunist revolt in Romania. Nor, admittedly, has China stood in the way of important enforcement actions undertaken by the UN in the cases of the Persian Gulf War, humanitarian intervention in Somalia, peacekeeping in the former Yugoslavia, and peace enforcement and peacebuilding in Haiti. Nevertheless, China's use of the threat of exercising its veto to gain economic or political concessions from the U.S., or simply to confirm the weight it carries in international politics, exemplifies the lengths to which Chinese leaders would go to promote China's self-interest at the expense of international order. In balancing these competing interests, China acts simultaneously to preserve the status quo (by exploiting the extant opportunities, rather than overtly seeking to revise or overthrow the status quo) and to undermine it (by pursuing economic gains and promoting the principle of absolute state sovereignty at the cost of arming bellicose states and hindering UN peacekeeping efforts). Paul Kennedy describes China's "balancing act" as follows: "Somewhat like the Germans earlier this century . . . the Chinese think deeply about 'encirclement' even as they simultaneously strive to enhance their place in the global system of power."[6]

Another way in which the maxi-mini strategy adopted by China plays out in international organizations is the Chinese leadership's willingness to tap the international environment for resources (monetary, technological, and human) necessary for its internal economic development aims, from the World Bank, and the UN, without permitting those organizations to impinge on its authority.[7] The importance of external sources of loans, investment, trade, technology transfers, and tourism became especially clear after Tiananmen, when international censure took the form of cutbacks or termination of those flows. The object of post-Tiananmen Chinese foreign policy has been to win the re-acceptance of the international community, as by taking modest measures to improve its human rights record and not blocking the vote (by abstaining) on Security Council Resolution 678, which authorized UN member states to take "all necessary means" to evict Iraq from Kuwait. In fact, much of China's foreign policy behavior after 1990, from pledges not to continue exporting missiles to, or sharing nuclear weapons technology and knowledge with, countries in the Middle East and South Asia, to abstentions in Security Council votes on a range of enforcement actions in the Persian Gulf, Somalia, former Yugoslavia, and Haiti, could be seen, in some measure, as part of a persistent effort to ingratiate itself with certain members of the international community, especially the United States and other members of the Western bloc.

The application of the maxi-mini strategy is also evident in the ambivalence China displays towards the United States. Ever since the late 1980s, when Chinese leaders perceived the increasing preponderance of the United States over the Soviet Union, China has been wary of American "hegemonism." Though it recognizes that the world has become somewhat multipolar, China treats America's foreign policy, especially in light of its resounding success over Iraq in the Persian Gulf War, with considerable suspicion. Ironically, China has been a beneficiary of the hegemonic role the United States has played in providing security in East Asia and its position as one of China's most important trading partners. America's peerless military strength and political prestige has inspired in the Chinese both a need to appease the world's sole remaining superpower for military, political, and economic reasons, and a fear of untrammeled American influence on the course of world events. As much as China resents the fact that the United States behaves heavy-handedly toward it, by threatening to remove its most-favored nation (MFN) trade status or impose trade sanctions on account of human rights abuses or intellectual property law violations, China views amity with the United States as an indispensable prerequisite for its goal of internal economic development. Chinese leaders have endeavored to extract as much economic and security benefit as they can from the United States while minimizing the amount of cooperation with the Americans necessary to achieve those ends.

From 1990 to 1995, China abstained 26 times, voted affirmatively with reservations 21 times, and voted affirmatively on the remainder of Security Council resolutions (of which a number were passed under Chapter VII), without exercising its veto even once. In what follows, I shall try to trace a pattern from all the resolutions in which China abstained and those Chapter VII resolutions in which it voted affirmatively (with or without reservations). A full list of relevant resolutions is given in the appendix to this chapter.

Abstentions on Resolutions Invoking Chapter VII Enforcement Powers

Of the 26 resolutions on which China abstained, 17 were explicitly enforcement measures taken by the Council under the authority vested in it under Chapter VII of the Charter. Of those 17, 3 concerned Iraq, 3 concerned the Federal Republic of Yugoslavia (Serbia and Montenegro), 6 concerned Bosnia-Herzegovina, 2 concerned Libya, 1 concerned Haiti, and 2 concerned Rwanda.

With regard to Iraq's invasion of Kuwait, China abstained on 3 Chapter VII resolutions:

1. Resolution 678 (1990) authorized "Member States cooperating with the Government of Kuwait, unless Iraq on or before 15 January 1991 fully implements . . . the foregoing resolutions, to use all necessary means to . . . restore international peace and security in the area."

During debate in the Security Council on the resolution, Chinese foreign minister Qian Qichen stated his government's hesitance in permitting the use of force against any member state: "In the draft resolution about to be voted on, the wording 'all necessary means' is used, which, in essence, permits the use of military action. This runs counter to the consistent position of the Chinese Government, namely, to try our utmost to seek a peaceful solution. Therefore, the Chinese delegation has difficulty voting in favor of this draft resolution.... Since China is in favor of [requiring Iraq to comply with Resolution 660 (1990) calling for an immediate withdrawal from Kuwait], China will not cast a negative vote on this draft resolution either."[8]

2. Resolution 686 (1991) set forth the conditions for the cessation of offensive combat operations by allied forces, including withdrawal of Iraq's annexation of Kuwait; reparations for damages to life and property in Kuwait; the release of all Kuwaiti and third country nationals; the cessation of all hostile actions against member states; the release of prisoners of war; and the meeting of military commanders on both sides to arrange armistice terms. The most obvious explanation for this abstention is China's explicit recognition that the provisions on the use of force of Resolution 678 "remain valid."[9]
3. Resolution 778 (1992) condemned Iraq's continued noncompliance with its obligations under previous resolutions; seized all previously frozen Iraqi assets abroad; provided for the use of Iraqi funds to offset the costs of UN activities concerning the elimination of weapons of mass destruction, humanitarian relief in Iraq, and other operations; and transferred all proceeds from Iraqi oil exported to other countries into an escrow account. On this matter, the Chinese delegate asserted, "we believe it is unnecessary to take so extraordinary a measure as the seizure of frozen assets abroad. . . . The seizure of a country's frozen assets abroad is a matter that constitutes the sovereignty of that country and involves complicated legal implications."[10]

In the case of Yugoslavia's involvement in the Bosnian civil war, China abstained on three Security Council resolutions that invoked Chapter VII authorization:

1. Resolution 757 (1992) applied sanctions on Yugoslavia encompassing trade (with the exception of medical supplies and foodstuffs), air transportation, diplomatic missions in Yugoslavia, and Yugoslav participation in sporting, scientific, technical, and cultural exchanges. In the Security Council, the Chinese delegate voiced the Chinese government's uneasiness with the application of sanctions against Yugoslavia, an

argument that would be reiterated frequently in subsequent debates: "We are concerned that sanctions will probably lead to further deterioration of the situation and create serious consequences. . . . We oppose the use of force."[11]

2. Resolution 787 (1992) widened trade restrictions specified by Resolution 757 to include crude oil, petroleum products, coal, energy-related equipment, iron, steel, other metals, chemicals, rubber, tires, vehicles, aircraft, and motors of all types; the inspection of all maritime shipping in order to ensure strict implementation of Resolutions 713 (1991) and 757; the deployment of observers on the borders of Bosnia-Herzegovina; and measures to ensure the safety of humanitarian assistance efforts.

3. Resolution 988 (1995) renewed a previous resolution easing sanctions on air transportation, ferry service, and participation in athletic and cultural events on Yugoslavia. China had supported the first resolution, 970 (1995), which eased sanctions against Yugoslavia, but decided to abstain on Resolution 988 because it felt the resolution was too restrictive in its conditions for the easing of sanctions, and did not suspend sanctions for a sufficient period, given Yugoslavia's efforts to bring the Bosnian Serbs to the negotiating table.[12]

With respect to the civil war in Bosnia, China abstained on six occasions when the Security Council debated taking Chapter VII measures:

1. Resolution 770 (1992) demanded unimpeded and continuous access to all prisons and detention centers by the Red Cross and other humanitarian organizations; and authorized "all parties and others concerned to take the necessary measures to ensure the safety of United Nations and other personnel engaged in the delivery of humanitarian assistance."

As with the use of Chapter VII authority to impose sanctions on Yugoslavia, the Chinese delegation took exception to the use of enforcement measures to secure UN and other personnel involved in the humanitarian mission in Bosnia: "We endorse the objective of facilitating the humanitarian relief work, as proclaimed in the resolution. But we cannot agree to the resolution's authorization of the use of force by member states, as it is precisely the continuous armed conflicts that are currently hindering the delivery of humanitarian assistance.... The broad authorization given to all States by the resolution to take all necessary measures is tantamount to issuing a blank check.... With regard to resolution 771 (1992), the Chinese delegation voted in favor solely out of humanitarian considerations. However, we deem it inappropriate to invoke Chapter VII of the Charter in this resolution.... It is our view that the invoking of Chapter VII should not constitute a precedent."[13] The delegate's last remark goes to show how assiduous the Chinese delegation was to cooperate with the other Big Five members while preserving its independence in future Security Council decisions.

2 & 3. Resolutions 781 (1992) and 816 (1993) established a ban on military flights over the territory of Bosnia-Herzegovina, with the exception of UN Protection Force (UNPROFOR) flights and flights taken in support of UN operations, and subsequently authorized member states (under Resolution 816), "acting nationally or through regional organizations or arrangements, to take, under the authority of the Security Council and subject to close coordination with the Secretary-General and UNPROFOR, all necessary measures in the airspace of the Republic of Bosnia and Herzegovina, in the event of further violations to ensure compliance with the ban on flights ... proportionate to the specific circumstances and the nature of the flights." This would be the basis upon which North Atlantic Treaty Organization (NATO) forces would engage and attack Bosnian Serb aircraft. On both resolutions, China made known its uneasiness with the authorization for the use of force.

Once again the Chinese delegation noted his government's principled objection to the use of Chapter VII powers: "We, in principle, do not oppose the establishment of a no-fly zone in Bosnia and Herzegovina with the consent of the parties concerned.... We wish to place on record that we have reservations on the invocation of Chapter VII to authorize countries to use force in implementing the no-fly zone."[14]

4 & 5. Resolutions 820 (1993) and 942 (1994) resolved to restrict economic activities (except in the case of medical supplies and foodstuffs) between member states and Bosnian Serb–held

territory of Bosnia; froze Bosnian Serb assets abroad; and ordered the inspection of all shipments of commodities and products destined for Bosnian Serb territory. Such measures were taken in order to compel the Bosnian Serbs to accept a political settlement of the conflict.

6. Resolution 998 (1995) demanded the release of UNPROFOR personnel held captive by Bosnian Serbs, and further augmented UNPROFOR by 12,500 troops. On this occasion, China reiterated its objection to UNPROFOR's peace enforcement mandate, which the Chinese believed to be in violation of the UN's basic peacekeeping principles and which they thought could possibly damage the credibility of the Security Council or the UN as a whole in the future.[15]

In response to the findings of an investigation made by the United States and the United Kingdom after the bombing of Pan Am Flight 103 and UTA Flight 772, the Security Council passed a number of resolutions on Libya, which had been linked to the bombings, two of which were Chapter VII resolutions on which China abstained from the vote:

1 and 2. Resolutions 748 (1992) and 883 (1993) imposed restrictions in the form of an embargo on air transportation and arms; downsizing of diplomatic missions to Libya; the freezing of Libyan government assets held abroad; and the expulsion from member states of Libyans previously found to be involved in terrorist activities.

As with the case of Yugoslavia, the Chinese delegate abstained from a vote on both occasions to impose sanctions on the basis of Chapter VII: "In principle, we do not support the Security Council imposing sanctions against Libya, because sanctions will not help settle the question, but will rather complicate the issue further, aggravate regional tension and have serious economic consequences for the countries concerned in the region."[16] One consideration for the Chinese delegation may have been the disruption of China's arms trade with Libya, which in fact became the focal point of controversy when American satellites confirmed the delivery of Chinese arms aboard a ship arriving in Libya on 17 April 1992, two days after the sanctions went into effect. China claimed that the ship entered Libyan waters before the sanctions were in force, and therefore did not constitute a breach of the resolution.

In order to restore the democratically elected president of Haiti, Jean-Bertrand Aristide, to his rightful place after he had been deposed, the Security Council resorted to Chapter VII measures that China abstained from affirming:

1. Resolution 940 (1994) authorized the formation of a multinational force to "use all necessary means to facilitate the departure from Haiti of the military leadership, consistent with the Governors Island Agreement, the prompt return of the legitimately elected President and the restoration of the legitimate authorities of the Government of Haiti"; the establishment of a secure environment for the UN Mission in Haiti (UNMIH) and of fair and free elections to be overseen by the Organization of American States (OAS); and the separation of the Haitian armed forces from the police and the professionalization of the latter.

In response to the peace enforcement and peacebuilding effort in Haiti, which the resolution at hand effectively justified, the Chinese delegate asserted: "We cannot agree to the provision in the draft resolution before us concerning the authorization for member states to adopt mandatory means under Chapter VII of the United Nations Charter to resolve the problem in Haiti. . . . The practice of the Council's authorizing certain member states to use force is even more disconcerting because this would obviously create a dangerous precedent."[17]

The last two Chapter VII resolutions in 1994 on which China abstained regarded the bloodbath in Rwanda as a result of fighting between the two major ethnic groups, the Hutus and the Tutsis:

1. Resolution 929 formed a multinational peacekeeping force to augment the French presence in Rwanda. China used this occasion to reaffirm the principles of Chapter VI of the Charter, which require the explicit approval of a UN peacekeeping operation by all parties to a conflict and which were not satisfied in the case of Rwanda. In the debate preceding the adoption of the resolution, the Chinese delegate reiterated the position of his government: "It is clear from the current situation that the action the draft resolution would authorize cannot guarantee the co-operation of the parties to that conflict. . . .

Hence, on the basis of the experience and lessons of the United Nations peacekeeping operation in Somalia, the Chinese delegation will abstain in the vote."[18]

2. Resolution 955 (1994) established an international tribunal to prosecute those responsible for genocide and other serious violations of international humanitarian law.

Like the cases of humanitarian assistance in Bosnia and peace enforcement and peacebuilding in Haiti, the case of enforcing international humanitarian law under the authority of Chapter VII disconcerted the Chinese delegation sufficiently enough that it abstained in the voting, reiterating the principled stand it made in the debate on Resolution 827 (1993), which set up an international tribunal charged with similar duties in Yugoslavia on Chapter VII grounds (on which China voted affirmatively). Hence, the Chinese delegation seemed unwilling to reaffirm the Yugoslav example in the case of Rwanda. Some considerations behind this change of heart may have been the absence of diplomatic pressure present in the former case, or a fear that two such resolutions would establish too great a precedent for international interference in a state's judicial sovereignty. Doubtless international criticism of its own human rights record played no small part in China's decision. The Chinese delegate argued in the debate on Resolution 827: "We have always held that, to avoid setting any precedent for abusing Chapter VII of the Charter, a prudent attitude should be adopted with regard to the establishment of an international tribunal by means of Security Council resolutions under Chapter VII. It is the consistent position of the Chinese delegation that an International Tribunal should be established by concluding a treaty so as to provide a solid legal foundation for it and ensure its effective functioning. . . . The International Tribunal established in the current manner can only be an ad hoc arrangement suited only to the special circumstances of the former Yugoslavia and shall not constitute a precedent."[19]

The pattern that emerges thus far with regard to China's abstentions on Chapter VII resolutions is one of Chinese reluctance to condone the use of the Security Council's enforcement authority to undertake military action against a member state (as in the case of Iraq), apply sanctions against a member state (as in the cases of Libya and Yugoslavia), undertake peace enforcement and peacebuilding (as in the case of Bosnia, Haiti, and Rwanda) and establish an international tribunal to prosecute widespread human rights abuses (as in the case of Rwanda). Yet, as we have seen in the case of Resolution 827, China is sometimes persuaded to affirm a resolution that violates its most cherished principle of the nonviolability of state sovereignty with nothing more than a reminder to the international community of its "principled position."

Abstentions on Non-Chapter VII Resolutions

The remaining nine Chinese abstentions, on resolutions passed on grounds other than Chapter VII, can be neatly divided into two nearly equal issue categories: first, resolutions that interfered with the internal affairs of a state without approval from all concerned parties, as required under Chapter VI; and second, resolutions that affected states and parties with which China has warm relations.

Into the first category fall Resolutions 688 (1991), 776 (1992), 855 (1993), 964 (1994), and 975 (1995). In the case of Resolution 688, the Security Council decided to add Iraq's repressive treatment of its minorities to the factors that made it a threat to international peace and security. This resolution carried with it an implicit enforcement mechanism, by asserting "Recalling of Article 2, paragraph 7, of the Charter," thereby implying that this action would fall into the category of intervention in the domestic jurisdiction of a state permitted by the application of enforcement measures under Chapter VII. In practice, the United States would use Resolution 688 as grounds to establish and enforce no-fly zones in northern and southern Iraq to protect Iraqi minorities in those regions. China abstained on the ground that while it was concerned about the refugee exodus from Iraq into neighboring states, the Security Council was interfering with what was rightly the internal matter of states.

Under Resolution 776, the Security Council authorized the enlargement of UNPROFOR's mandate and strength in Bosnia. As in the case of Resolution 688, Resolution 766 carried an implicit enforcement mechanism by grounding its authority in the implementation of Resolution 770 (which had been passed under Chapter VII) by facilitating the humanitarian mission in Bosnia-Herzegovina. China's reservation arose from the subtle linkages of enforcement measures and the peacekeeping operation: "In principle, the Chinese delegation does not object to the strengthening of humanitarian-assistance activities, but the resolution at issue established a link between the enlargement of the mandate of UNPROFOR and the implementation of Security Council resolution 770. . . . Security Council resolution 770 . . . is a mandatory action taken under Chapter VII of the United Nations Charter. We are concerned that linking this resolution with resolution 770 . . . will change the non-mandatory nature of UNPROFOR as the United Nations peacekeeping operation."[20]

Resolution 855 demanded that Yugoslavia reconsider its "refusal to allow the continuation of the activities of the Conference on Security and Co-operation in Europe (CSCE) missions in Kosovo, Sandjak, and Vojvodina and cooperate with the CSCE by taking the practical steps needed for the resumption of the activities of these missions and agree to an increase in the number of monitors as decided by the CSCE." China saw this as undue interference in the internal matters of Yugoslavia, and went on to assert, "Preventive diplomacy, as part of the pacific settlement of disputes embodied in Chapter VI of the Charter, should be carried out at the explicit request, or with the prior consent, of the States and parties concerned. It should never be imposed against their will."[21]

In Resolutions 964 and 975, the Security Council strengthened and deployed the UN Mission in Haiti (UNMIH). China had abstained on the resolution that had established UNMIH (Resolution 940, passed under Chapter VII), and reminded the Council once again that it "opposed interference in the internal affairs of other countries and the use or threat of the use of force in international relations. We expounded this position when the Council adopted resolution 940 . . . which authorized military action in Haiti. Still less should resolution 964 . . . which had just been adopted, be understood as an affirmation of this so-called formula."[22] It is difficult to say how much Haiti's support for Taiwanese membership in the UN influenced China's decisions. In a later resolution, 1048 (1996), the Chinese seemed close to exercising their veto to block extension of the UNMIH in retaliation for the invitation of Taiwan's vice president, Li Yuan-zu, to the inauguration of Haiti's new president in Port-au-Prince on 7 February 1996. In the end, China used the veto threat so as to reduce the number of UNMIH troops from 1,900 to 1,200. Because the reduced force was thought to be insufficient for the task of peacekeeping, Canada agreed to make up for the shortfall of 700 troops at its own expense to salvage the mission.[23]

Within the second category of non–Chapter VII resolutions on which China abstained are Resolutions 777 (1992), 792 (1992), 821 (1993), and 825 (1993). Resolutions 777 and 821 dealt with

Yugoslavia's status within the United Nations and its organs. In the former case, the Security Council prevented Yugoslavia from automatically taking the former Socialist Republic of Yugoslavia's seat in the UN, leaving it up to the General Assembly to decide the case. In the latter, the Council precluded the participation of Yugoslavia in the work of the Economic and Social Council. In the debate on these resolutions, China made note of its opposition to unnecessarily alienating Yugoslavia. China's stance must have been in some way affected by Yugoslavia's influential position in the Non-Aligned Movement, a group that China had courted in the 1970s.

Another party that China seemed anxious not to isolate was the Khmer Rouge, against which the Security Council applied sanctions under Resolution 792, owing to the Khmer Rouge's intransigence in fulfilling its obligations under the Paris Agreements with Prince Sihanouk and its attacks on the UN Transitional Authority in Cambodia (UNTAC). The Chinese delegate indicated his unwillingness to punish any single party in Cambodia: "Instead of helping to solve the problems, sanctions will further increase differences and sharpen contradictions and could consequently lead to new, complicated problems."[24]

The Security Council also passed Resolution 825, which called on North Korea, one of China's oldest allies, to reconsider its withdrawal from the Nuclear Non-Proliferation Treaty (NPT) in 1993 and to comply with its safeguards agreement with the International Atomic Energy Agency (IAEA). Preferring not to pressure North Korea, China argued the nuclear issue "should . . . be settled properly through the direct dialogue and consultation between the Democratic People's Republic of Korea and the three other parties concerned [the IAEA, the U.S., and South Korea]."[25]

From the pattern of China's abstentions in non–Chapter VII resolutions, it is clear that when the Council sought to undertake operations putatively under Chapter VI authority (such as in the cases of UNPROFOR in Bosnia, the CSCE special mission in Yugoslavia, and peace enforcement in Rwanda), China has been especially insistent that all parties to a conflict approve such action (as required by the Charter). Similarly, when the Council adopted resolutions with a subtle hint of Chapter VII enforcement authority, by making reference to the implementation of previous resolutions passed under explicit Chapter VII authority, China resisted the slippage of peacekeeping or other types of operations into enforcement action (as in the cases of the refugee crisis in Iraq and the no-fly zone over Bosnia).

A much less conclusive finding is that in the case of the remaining non–Chapter VII resolutions on which China abstained, its motivations had more to do with specific diplomatic-political considerations than with foreign policy principles. Yet there is a clear pattern of states or parties that China sought to shield from what it perceived to be unequal treatment by the Security Council: Yugoslavia, the Khmer Rouge, and North Korea. Of course, China's foreign policy principle of absolute state sovereignty benefits itself as much as its allies and friends, such as those just mentioned. Hence, it may not be important to decide whether China's primary motivation was one of principle or politics.

Chapter VII
Resolutions that China Affirmed, with or without Reservations

Before drawing any conclusions about China's behavior in the Security Council on the basis of its abstentions, it is necessary briefly to examine the resolutions with which China concurred, of which a number passed under Chapter VII. In what follows, I shall consider those Chapter VII resolutions, making note of when China agreed with or without reservations.

All subsequent resolutions on which China joined the other permanent members in voting and yet expressed reservations were passed under Chapter VII. At the same time, on a large number of occasions China affirmed a Chapter VII resolution without expressing any reservations. On the occasions China made note of its reservations, it did so on two ostensible bases: first, that the resolution unduly impinged on the internal affairs of a state, and that there was a danger of a peacekeeping operation sliding into enforcement action; and second, that the resolution was adopted given the "exceptional circumstances" of the situation, and should not therefore "constitute a precedent." On the occasions when China did not make any reservations, there was little indication of its motivations, given the fact that the Chinese delegate remained silent during the official debate. One can surmise something about the intentions behind the affirmative vote on certain issues regarding Iraq, for example, but on others—in Bosnia and Haiti—it is more difficult, especially in light of abstentions on similar issues in previous and subsequent votes.

The first category of votes, in which China voted affirmatively on Chapter VII resolutions with reservations, contains 21 resolutions: 771

(1992), 794 (1992), 814 (1993), 827 (1993), 836 (1993), 841 (1993), 871 (1993), 875 (1993), 900 (1994), 908 (1994), 913 (1994), 914 (1994), 917 (1994), 944 (1994), 958 (1994), 970 (1995), 990 (1995), 994 (1995), 1004 (1995), 1009 (1995), and 1031 (1995). The principal reason behind China's reservations on a number of these resolutions was the slippery slope between peacekeeping operations and enforcement measures. In Resolutions 836, 871, 900, 908, 913, 914, 958, and 1004, UNPROFOR's size and mandate were gradually expanded, to allow the use of force to protect the safe areas in Bosnia. In official debate the Chinese delegate expressed his uneasiness with linking UNPROFOR's peacekeeping mandate with enforcement authority; in particular, China had reservations with the possibility that air power would be used not simply for self-defense, but for punitive and preemptive purposes.[26] Furthermore, the Chinese were concerned with the possibility that the peacekeeping force would become a party to the conflict in Bosnia.[27]

In official debate on Resolutions 794 and 814, the Chinese delegate made note of his government's hesitance to lend the UNOSOM peacekeeping operation a veneer of mandatory enforcement action, as the resolution does, and asserted that China voted affirmatively with the understanding that such action "should not constitute a precedent for United Nations peace-keeping operations."[28] The two resolutions dealt with the situation in Somalia by augmenting the UN Operation in Somalia (UNOSOM); authorizing the Secretary-General and member states "to use all necessary means to establish as soon as possible a secure environment for humanitarian relief operations in Somalia"; and, in the case of the latter resolution, enabling UNOSOM II forces to help implement the arms embargo instituted by Resolution 733 (1992). Resolution 794 marked the first time ever the Security Council included humanitarian disasters not of human making a condition that constituted a threat to international peace and security.

China also indicated reservations to Chapter VII resolutions dealing with international human rights tribunals in the former Yugoslavia. Resolution 771 condemned violations of international humanitarian law, especially the practice of ethnic cleansing, and called for nongovernmental organizations and states to collate information on human rights violations. China succeeded in deleting from the draft a paragraph referring to a commission of human rights, arguing that the Security Council's jurisdiction did not extend to matters of monitoring human rights violations.[29] Resolution 827 established an international tribunal to prosecute violations of international humanitarian law in the former

Yugoslavia on the basis of Chapter VII. As it would remind the Council again in the future, in the vote on Resolution 955 regarding Rwanda, China expressed its opposition to establishing a war crimes tribunal on the basis of Chapter VII, rather than by statute. To do so, the Chinese delegate argued, would impinge on the judicial sovereignty of states; his government's affirmative vote was made in view of the special circumstances presented in the case of the former Yugoslavia. China's hesitance to condone UN action with respect to alleged war crimes in Bosnia is consistent with its long-standing insistence on treating human rights as an attribute of state sovereignty and therefore beyond the reach of legitimate interference.

China invoked special circumstances in its affirmative votes on Resolutions 875, 917, and 944, which imposed sanctions, then an international embargo, and finally deployed an advance team of UNMIH. The Chinese delegate stated the position of his government: "The sanctions regime contained in this resolution is, in the absence of other effective measures, an exceptional step taken under highly unique circumstances now prevailing in Haiti and one which should not constitute any precedent."[30] When it came to deploying a peacekeeping mission to Haiti, China reiterated its objection to interference in the internal affairs of states and the resort or threat of the use of force in international relations.[31]

In Resolutions 990, 994, 1009, and 1031, the UN first authorized a peacekeeping mission to Croatia (UNCRO), demanded that warring factions cease offensive military action and respect UNCRO's status and mandate, and finally authorized a multinational implementation force (IFOR) to take over UNPROFOR's peacekeeping responsibilities in Bosnia after the signing of the Basic Peace Agreement. China objected to the invocation of Chapter VII enforcement powers for peacekeeping missions in Croatia and Bosnia (after the peace agreement had been signed) because such missions could have been deployed under Chapter VI, since they had the approval of domestic parties. In light of the duration and brutality of the conflict in Bosnia, though, some members of the Security Council no doubt thought that a traditional Chapter VI peacekeeping force might be unequal to the task. Chapter VII permits member states and a peacekeeping force greater scope for the use of force and requires a Security Council vote to end the mission, whereas Chapter VI would permit a peacekeeping force to act only out of self-defense and the mission would have to leave upon the request of a domestic party.

China also indicated its reservations to the treatment of Yugoslavia after its efforts to get the Bosnian Serbs to negotiate a peace agreement. In return for its assistance with regard to the Bosnia Serbs, the Security Council passed Resolution 970, which eased sanctions on air transportation, ferry service, and participation in athletic and cultural exchanges. In the debate over the resolution, China restated its objection to sanctions against Yugoslavia (it had abstained twice on two prior resolutions, 757 and 820, imposing sanctions) on the grounds that the restrictions were still unjustified and that more encouragement should be given to Yugoslavia for its cooperation.[32]

There are 59 votes in the second category, in which China backed Chapter VII resolutions without reservations. Part of the difficulty in divining the reasons behind China's full backing of Chapter VII resolutions (with the exception of those with regard to Iraq and Kuwait) is that the Chinese delegate made no indication of his government's position during official debate. In the case of Resolutions 661 (1990), 664 (1990), 665 (1990), 666 (1990), 667 (1990), 670 (1990), 674 (1990), 677 (1990), 687 (1991), 689 (1991), 692 (1991), 699 (1991), 700 (1991), 705 (1991), 706 (1991), 707 (1991), 712 (1991), 715 (1991), 806 (1993), 833 (1993), 899 (1994), and 949 (1994), China consistently exhibited its willingness to cooperate with the American-led effort to punish blatant Iraqi aggression by voting affirmatively on resolutions dealing with the international embargo of Iraq; condemnation of Iraqi actions taken against diplomatic personnel, Kuwaitis, and third state nationals; establishment of conditions for a formal cease-fire, creation of the UN Iraq-Kuwait Observer Mission (UNIKOM) after the armistice had been signed; destruction of Iraq's nuclear, chemical, and biological weapons capabilities; creation of a compensation fund for Iraqis and Kuwaitis; and the demarcation of the Iraq-Kuwait border. Iraq would be the only issue on which the Chinese would make no mention of their hesitance to take enforcement action against a member state, with the exception of Resolution 678 (in which it abstained). On Resolution 670, foreign minister Qian noted China's foreign policy principle of preferring the peaceful resolution of disputes over the use of force, though his statement in official debate was couched in lofty conceptions: "In our view, it has been proved by post-war history that the kind of order that is based on military might and the use of force will not stand in the end, where the five principles [of peaceful co-existence] . . . are full of vitality."[33]

Another category of votes in which the Chinese expressed no reservations was on the easing of sanctions, which is consistent with its principled position against taking Chapter VII action against member states. In Resolutions 760 (1992), 1003 (1995), 1015 (1995), and 1021 (1995), some sanctions were gradually lifted against Yugoslavia, for humanitarian reasons as well as in return for Yugoslav cooperation in the Bosnian peace efforts. Resolution 919 (1994) lifted the arms embargo and other restrictions against South Africa after the end of apartheid. Resolution 861 (1993) suspended sanctions against Haiti once the military government agreed to relinquish its power, though sanctions were later reimposed when the military failed to live up to the Governor's Island Agreement. China's affirmative vote without reservations on the reimposition of sanctions on Haiti, in Resolution 873 (1993), is at variance with its previous objections to taking punitive measures, such as sanctions, against member states. In recognition of the deleterious effect sanctions can have on civilian welfare, sanctions were also partially lifted in Resolution 967 (1994) and Resolution 986 (1995) in the cases of Bosnia and Iraq respectively. Finally, the arms embargo against Rwanda was lifted, under Resolutions 1005 (1995) and 1011 (1995), once the Rwandan government reestablished domestic order.

On a number of other issues, China's affirmative vote without reservations is inconsistent with its usual insistence of refraining from taking Chapter VII measures to enforce embargoes or authorize peacekeeping missions. China acquiesced to resolutions imposing an arms embargo on Yugoslavia (Resolutions 713 [1991] and 724 [1991]), Somalia (Resolution 733 [1992]), and Liberia (Resolution 788 [1992]). Furthermore, China authorized the extension of mandates for several peacekeeping operations without mentioning objections it previously had on those missions. Resolutions 819 (1993), 824 (1993), 844 (1993), 859 (1993), 869 (1993), 870 (1993), 941 (1994), 943 (1994), 982 (1995), 987 (1995), and 1026 (1995) dealt with the extension of UNPROFOR's mandate and the creation of safe areas in which UNPROFOR was authorized to use force in order to protect itself. Resolutions concerning the UN Angola Verification Mission (UNAVEM) (Resolution 864 [1993]), the UN Assistance Mission for Rwanda (UNAMIR) (Resolution 918 [1994]), UNOSOM (Resolutions 837 [1993], 878 [1993], 886 [1993], 897 [1994], 923 [1994], and 954 [1994]), and the replacement of UNCRO by a transitional peacekeeping force (Resolution 1025 [1995]) also contained Chapter VII enforcement authority for peacekeeping missions to which China would be expected to object.

China approved one other resolution, 910 (1994), permitting the Secretary-General to aerially survey an area of Chad previously occupied by Libya in order to judge its suitability for an observer mission. The absence of any Chinese reservations on this resolution is at odds with previous resolutions in which the Security Council took enforcement action against Libya. Although the resolution impinged on Libyan airspace, China would not have felt the necessity to express reservations since the resolution did not entail the use of force.

An Assessment of China's Voting Behavior in the Security Council

The general pattern of China's voting behavior that emerges is one of a reluctance to countenance Chapter VII actions, since it abstained or expressed reservations on 38 out of 97 Chapter VII resolutions passed by the Security Council in the period from the Iraqi invasion of Kuwait in 1990 until the end of 1994. The most obvious explanation for such behavior is the desire to retain a status of neutrality on serious threats to international peace and security. As a result of its neutral orientation, the Chinese are able to balance their material interests with their foreign policy principles.

Chinese decision makers have attempted to steer their ship of state on an uneasy course between the necessities of their future economic prosperity and the dictates of their principled position of resisting superpower hegemonism. In order to promote its internal economic development goals, China has found international sources of capital, labor, and technology to be indispensable. Since much of this support had been cut after the Tiananmen Square massacre of 1989, subsequent Chinese foreign policy was bent on persuading the international community to invite it back into the fold. The Persian Gulf war became the ideal opportunity to demonstrate its willingness to act responsibly in world affairs. Moreover, the Gulf War diverted the attention of the international community from China's human rights abuses to the more reprehensible acts of aggression committed by Iraq against Kuwait. China's support of all ten Security Council resolutions preceding the authorization of the use of force in Resolution 678 may be understood in the light of China's desire to regain the approval of the international community, especially that of the U.S., since American sanctions were especially deleterious to the Chinese economy.

As a reward for China's abstention in the Security Council during the vote on Resolution 678, on 30 November 1990 (a day after the passage of Resolution 678), the Bush administration invited Chinese foreign minister Qian to Washington after almost a year of a ban on high-level exchanges with the Chinese government instituted as a response to Tiananmen. The insistence of the U.S. government that these "contacts" were not formal "exchanges" hardly diminished the significance of Qian's meeting with President Bush and Secretary of State James Baker. An equally important coup for the Chinese was Washington's abstention, only four days later, on a World Bank vote extending a $114.3 million loan (of which about $50 million came from the Bank's soft-credit window, the International Development Association) for the Rural Industries (or "Spark") project in China, the first time such a loan had been approved by the World Bank for purposes other than reasons of "basic human needs (BHN)." Since Tiananmen, the administration (under considerable Congressional pressure) had asserted it would only support loans to China for reasons of BHN; e.g., earthquake relief, rural development, and vocational training.[34] Although Washington had maintained substantial progress on human rights as a precondition for resuming non-BHN loans, the World Bank vote came at a time while China was in the process of launching prosecutions against leaders of the pro-democracy movement. For China, both Qian's visit to Washington and the World Bank's approval of a non-BHN loan were manifestations of the value of independence (or neutrality) in an era when China's association with the United States in the "strategic triangle" of the 1970s had lost its salience.

Of course, China could not possibly expect rewards each and every time it cooperated with the United States, given the considerable political-diplomatic power the latter could exert in achieving its foreign policy objectives. In the case of Resolution 748, for instance, after sustained American arm twisting China agreed to drop its threat of vetoing any resolution ordering sanctions against Libya.[35] The power that the United States can bring to bear in world affairs is the source of both great esteem and great wariness for the Chinese. Whereas cooperation with America is valued for the sake of remaining on good terms with the world's most powerful country, as well as for material benefits that China can sometimes manage to extract, the threat of unchecked American hegemonic behavior is an important consideration in the formulation of Chinese foreign policy. China has expressed its opposition to American adventurism by abstaining on votes authorizing the

UN or certain member states to use force in addressing threats to international peace and security (as in the cases of Iraq, Bosnia, Somalia, Haiti, and Rwanda). In doing so, China is not exhibiting a desire to revise the current international order so much as to reduce America's political and diplomatic influence in an increasingly multipolar world. The Security Council's ability to impose harsh sanctions (as in the cases of Yugoslavia, Libya, and Haiti) on renegade states would also be considered by the Chinese as an avenue the United States and its allies may take to impose its will on weaker states.

Beijing's willingness to compromise with Washington should not, therefore, be overestimated. Whereas the invocation of foreign policy principles should also be treated with some skepticism, in China's case the Five Principles of Peaceful Co-existence are closely linked with its fear of hegemonic power. Although China has been reduced to reiterating its Westphalian view of state sovereignty time and again in abstentions or reservations to affirmative votes cast in the Security Council, China remains the preeminent defender of a conception of absolute state sovereignty that has increasingly eroded as a result of popular notions of sovereignty. Hence, China's espousal of the Five Principles can be seen as having as much to do with the preservation of its own power and influence in international relations as with the preservation of its domestic political order. For a regime forced to take harsh measures to counter the centrifugal force of regional economic interdependence, the trend of international intrusion into the internal affairs of states, particularly on humanitarian grounds, is bound to cause consternation. In fact, China's threat of veto gains credibility because of the very real interest China has in preventing international interference in its own domestic affairs and those of its allies. The promotion of such principles to gain the good favor and admiration of non-aligned states was an additional benefit China has exploited only since the 1970s. To retain the allegiance of the Third World while at the same time failing to prevent the application of force against Iraq, China abstained so as to gain the advantages of cooperating with the United States while divesting itself of full responsibility for the use of force.[36] This is as good an example as any of what Kim labeled China's maxi-mini strategy.

China's votes with regard to resolutions passed against its erstwhile allies needs little explanation. Most recently, China held up a resolution condemning Cuba for its downing of two American civilian aircraft flying in or near Cuban airspace until the United States agreed to tone down the language of the resolution.[37] It would be foolish to expect the permanent members of the Security Council to resist using their influence and veto power to shield important diplomatic allies. After all, this was the motivation behind America's consistent opposition to resolutions condemning Israel for its actions against Palestinians in the occupied territories and against its Arab neighbors.

Judging from the present state of Chinese foreign relations, one cannot escape the conclusion that Chinese foreign policy has, on the whole, been successful in achieving its primary objectives. As a result of its cooperation with the United States and the West in the Security Council during the Persian Gulf War, China made its reentry into the international community after more than a year of imposed isolation after Tiananmen Square. Moreover, China succeeded in receiving a tangible reward of a World Bank loan soon after its noninterference in the passage of Resolution 678. Normal economic relations with most countries have since resumed. China persuaded the United States to renew its MFN status and consider it for charter membership (which it eventually did not get) in the General Agreement on Tariffs and Trade's successor organization, the World Trade Organization. Of course, these rewards came as a result not only of China's Security Council behavior, but of other instances of cooperation as well, such as its agreement to abide by the Non-Proliferation Treaty and the Missile Technology Control Regime in late 1991. Although China has far to go to gain the complete approval of the international community, as the demise of its bid to host the 2000 Olympics might suggest, it has come a long way in mitigating the effects of its repressive human rights policy.

China may also be credited with deftly using the UN, and especially the Security Council, to promote what it calls the new international economic and political order, which is nothing much more than a restatement of the mid-seventeenth century Westphalian notion of absolute state sovereignty. The authority of the UN is one instrument states may use to promulgate a certain conception of international order, an opportunity that both China and the West have seized. In resisting (though only weakly thus far) American-led attempts to use the authority of the Security Council to bring humanitarian disasters under the category of threats to international peace and security, China goes some way in preventing UN-sanctioned use of force and humanitarian intervention by the Western powers from becoming the regular practice of states. (Its assertion that the relevant resolutions should not be seen as constituting a precedent is important in that regard.) This achievement, as tenuous as it might be, serves China's national interest in preserving an external environment conducive to its own internal development goals just as much as it promotes China's world order views. The threat to use its veto power in the Security Council has been a central element in this strategy.

APPENDIX

Chinese Abstentions on All Resolutions, and Affirmative Votes on Chapter VII Resolutions in the Security Council, 1990-1995

(All other countries voting affirmatively, unless otherwise noted)

Resolution no.	Affirmative Without Reservations	Affirmative With Reservations	Abstain
661 (1990)	Iraq—economic sanctions [*Ch. VII*] (Cuba and Yemen abstaining)		
664	Iraq—safety of third-state nations in Iraq and Kuwait [*Ch. VII*]		
665	Iraq—shipping embargo [*Ch. VII*] (Cuba and Yemen abstaining)		
666	Iraq and Kuwait—situation regarding food availability [*Ch. VII*] (Cuba and Yemen against)		
667	Iraq—condemnation of Iraqi actions against diplomatic premises and personnel in Kuwait [*Ch. VII*]		
670	Iraq—air transport embargo [*Ch. VII*](Cuba against)		
674	Iraq—treatment of third state nationals, Kuwaitis, and diplomatic personnel [*Ch. VII*] (Cuba and Yemen abstaining)		
677	Iraq and Kuwait—Iraqi attempts to alter demographic composition of Kuwait [*Ch. VII*]—		

China's Voting Pattern in the Security Council 109

Resolution no.	Affirmative Without Reservations	Affirmative With Reservations	Abstain
678			Iraq—deadline for withdrawal from Kuwait [*Ch. VII*] (Cuba and Yemen against)
686 (1991)			Iraq—conditions for the cessation of combat operations [*Ch. VII*] (Cuba against and India Yemen abstaining)
687	Iraq—conditions for formal cease-fire [*Ch. VII*] (Cuba against, and Ecuador and Yemen abstaining)		
688			Iraq—Iraqi civilian population (Cuba, Yemen, and Zimbabwe against, and India abstaining)
689	Iraq—creation of UNIKOM [*Ch. VII*]		
692	Iraq—establishment of compensation fund [*Ch. VII*] (Cuba abstaining)		
699	Iraq—destruction of nuclear, chemical, and biological weapons [*Ch. VII*]		
700	Iraq—implementation of arms embargo [*Ch. VII*]		
705	Iraq—compensation to be paid [*Ch. VII*]		
706	Iraq—conditions for the resumption of petroleum exports [*Ch. VII*] (Cuba against and Yemen abstaining)		
707	Iraq—destruction of nuclear, chemical, and biological weapons [*Ch. VII*]		
712	Iraq—release of funds to meet Iraq's humanitarian needs [*Ch. VII*] (Cuba against and Yemen abstaining)		
713	Yugoslavia—arms embargo [*Ch. VII*]		

Resolution no.	Affirmative Without Reservations	Affirmative With Reservations	Abstain
715	Iraq—reaffirms IAEA mandate to monitor and verify Iraq's nuclear capability [*Ch. VII*]		
724	Yugoslavia—implementation of arms embargo [*Ch. VII*]		
733 (1992)	Somalia—arms embargo and provision of humanitarian assistance [*Ch. VII*]		
748			Libya—cooperation with legal measures concerning Pan Am Flight 103 [*Ch. VII*] (Ecuador, Morocco, India, and Zimbabwe abstaining)
757			Yugoslavia—sanctions [*Ch. VII*] (Zimbabwe abstaining)
760	Yugoslavia—partial lifting of sanctions for humanitarian reasons [*Ch. VII*]		
770			Bosnia—humanitarian assistance [*Ch. VII*] (India and Zimbabwe abstaining)
771		Bosnia—violations of international humanitarian law [*Ch. VII*]	
776			Bosnia—enlargement of UNPROFOR (India and Zimbabwe abstain)
777			Yugoslavia—members status within UN (India and Zimbabwe abstain)
778			Iraq—noncompliance with previous resolution [*Ch. VII*]
781			Bosnia—military no-fly zone [*Ch. VII*]
787			Yugoslavia—embargo on commodities and products [*Ch. VII*] (Zimbabwe abstaining)
788	Liberia—arms embargo [*Ch. VII*]		

China's Voting Pattern in the Security Council 111

Resolution no.	Affirmative Without Reservations	Affirmative With Reservations	Abstain
792			Cambodia—implementation of peace process
794		Somalia—security measures for humanitarian assistance operation [*Ch. VII*]	
806 (1993)	Iraq—UNIKOM terms of reference [*Ch. VII*]		
814		Somalia—reconciliation process [*Ch. VII*]	
816			Bosnia—military no-fly zone [*Ch. VII*]
819	Bosnia—creation of safe area [*Ch. VII*]		
820			Bosnia—measures to bring Bosnian Serbs to peace process [*Ch. VII*] (Russia abstaining)
821			Yugoslavia—participation in Economic and Social Council (Russia abstaining)
824	Bosnia—creation of safe areas [*Ch. VII*]		
825			North Korea—decision to withdraw from NPT (Pakistan abstaining)
827		Yugoslavia—international war crimes tribunal [*Ch. VII*]	
833	Iraq—demarcation of Iraq-Kuwait boundary [*Ch. VII*]		
836		Bosnia—authorization for UNPROFOR to use force in replying to bombardments of safe areas [*Ch. VII*] (Pakistan and Venezuela abstaining)	
837	Somalia—condemnation of attacks on UNOSOM II personnel [*Ch. VII*]		

Resolution no.	Affirmative Without Reservations	Affirmative With Reservations	Abstain
841		Haiti—oil and arms embargo [*Ch. VII*]	
844	Bosnia—reinforcement of UNPROFOR [*Ch. VII*]		
855			Yugoslavia—refusal to allow CSCE special missions into Bosnia
859	Bosnia—call for cease-fire [*Ch. VII*]		
861	Haiti—suspension of sanctions [*Ch. VII*]		
864	Angola—extension of UNAVEM II mandate and possible sanctions against UNITA [*Ch. VII*]		
869	Bosnia—extension of UNPROFOR mandate [*Ch. VII*]		
870	Bosnia—extension of UNPROFOR mandate [*Ch. VII*]		
871		Bosnia—extension of UNPROFOR mandate [*Ch. VII*]	
873	Haiti—reimposition of sanctions [*Ch. VII*]		
875		Haiti—implementation of sanctions [*Ch. VII*]	
878	Somalia—extension of UNOSOM II mandate [*Ch. VII*]		
883			Libya—sanctions [*Ch. VII*] (Djibouti, Morocco, and Pakistan abstaining)
886	Somalia—extension of UNOSOM II mandate [*Ch. VII*]		
897 (1994)	Somalia—extension of UNOSOM II mandate [*Ch. VII*]		
899	Iraq—compensation to Iraqis for assets remaining in Kuwait after demarcation [*Ch. VII*]		

China's Voting Pattern in the Security Council 113

Resolution no.	Affirmative Without Reservations	Affirmative With Reservations	Abstain
900		Bosnia—humanitarian mission to Sarajevo [*Ch.VII*]	
908		Bosnia—extension of UNPROFOR mandate and increase of personnel [*Ch. VII*]—	
910	Libya—authorization for UN aircraft to fly Secretary-General's reconnaissance team over Libya [*Ch. VII*]		
913		Bosnia—UNPROFOR to monitor safe area [*Ch. VII*]	
914		Bosnia—increase of UNPROFOR personnel [*Ch. VII*]	
917		Haiti—sanctions [*Ch. VII*]	
918	Rwanda—expansion of UNAMIR mandate and imposition of arms embargo [*Ch. VII*]		
919	South Africa—termination of arms embargo and other restrictions [*Ch. VII*]		
923	Somalia—extension of UNOSOM II mandate [*Ch. VII*]		
929			Rwanda—temporary multinational relief operation [*Ch. VII*] (Brazil, New Zealand, Nigeria, and Pakistan abstaining)
940			Haiti—multinational force to restore democracy [*Ch. VII*] (Brazil abstaining, with Rwanda not present)
941	Bosnia—violations of international humanitarian law by Bosnian Serbs [*Ch. VII*]		

Resolution no.	Affirmative Without Reservations	Affirmative With Reservations	Abstain
942			Bosnia—measures against Bosnian Serb territory [*Ch. VII*]
943	Bosnia—closure of Yugoslav/Bosnia border except for supplies for essential humanitarian needs [*Ch. VII*] (Djibouti and Pakistan against, and Nigeria and Rwanda abstaining)		
944		Haiti—deployment of UNMIH advance team [*Ch. VII*] (Brazil and Russia abstaining)	
949	Iraq—demand withdrawal of Iraqi troops from southern Iraq [*Ch. VII*]		
954	Somalia—extension of UNOSOM II mandate [*Ch. VII*]		
955			Rwanda—international tribunal [*Ch. VII*] (Rwanda against)
958		Bosnia and Croatia—authorization to use air power to protect safe areas [*Ch. VII*]	
964			Haiti—advance team of UNMIH (Russia abstaining)
967	Bosnia—partial lifting of sanctions for humanitarian reasons [*Ch. VII*]		
970 (1995)		Yugoslavia—partial easing of sanctions [*Ch. VII*] (Russia abstaining)	
975			Haiti—deployment of UNMIH
982	Bosnia—extension of UNPROFOR mandate [*Ch. VII*]		
986	Iraq—partial resumption of petroleum exports [*Ch. VII*]		

China's Voting Pattern in the Security Council 115

Resolution no.	Affirmative Without Reservations	Affirmative With Reservations	Abstain
987	Bosnia—demand that warring factions refrain from threatening UNPROFOR [*Ch. VII*]		
988			Yugoslavia—75-days suspension of some sanctions [*Ch. VII*] (Russia abstaining)
990		Croatia—UNCRO mandate [*Ch. VII*]	
992	Yugoslavia—restrictions on navigation on Danube river [*Ch. VII*]		
994		Croatia—demands status and mandate of UNCRO be respected, and Croatia cease offensive military action [*Ch. VII*]	
998			Bosnia—demand for release of UNPROFOR hostages held by Bosnian Serbs, and increase of UNPROFOR personnel [*Ch. VII*] (Russia abstaining)
1003	Yugoslavia—temporary lifting of some sanctions [*Ch. VII*] (Russia abstaining)		
1004		Bosnia—UNPROFOR measures to protect safe area [*Ch. VII*]	
1005	Rwanda—partial lifting of arms embargo [*Ch. VII*]		
1009		Croatia—call for Croatia to cease military action [*Ch. VII*]	
1011	Rwanda—lifting of arms embargo on government [*Ch. VII*]		
1015	Yugoslavia—temporary suspension of some sanctions [*Ch. VII*]		
1021	Yugoslavia—conditions of lifting of arms embargo [*Ch. VII*] (Russia abstaining)		

Resolution no.	Affirmative Without Reservations	Affirmative With Reservations	Abstain
1025	Croatia—termination of UNCRO, to be replaced by transitional peacekeeping force [*Ch. VII*]		
1026	Bosnia—extension of UNPROFOR mandate [*Ch. VII*]		
1031		Bosnia—authorization for IFOR [*Ch. VII*]	

NOTES

1. Anjali V. Patil, *The UN Veto in World Affairs, 1946 - 1990: A Complete Record and Case Histories of the Security Council's Veto* (London: Mansell, 1992), p. 486.
2. Samuel S. Kim, "China and the Third World," in Kim, ed., *China and the World: Chinese Foreign Relations in the Post - Cold War Era,* 3rd ed. (Boulder, Col.: Westview Press, 1994), pp. 144, 161.
3. Kim, "China and the World in Theory and Practice," in Kim, ed., *China and the World,* p. 32.
4. Kim, "China and the Third World," pp. 132-33.
5. Ibid., pp. 141-42. See also Kim, "China In and Out of the Changing World Order," World Studies Program Occasional Paper No. 21 (Princeton, N.J.: Center of International Studies, Princeton University, 1991), p. 76.
6. Paul Kennedy, *The Rise and Fall of the Great Powers: Economic Change and Military Conflict from 1500 to 2000* (New York: Vintage, 1989), p. 447.
7. Thomas W. Robinson, "Interdependence in China's Foreign Relations," in Kim, ed., *China and the World,* pp. 191-2.
8. United Nations Document S/PV.2963, pp.62-63.
9. Hwei-Ling Huo, "Patterns of Behavior in China's Foreign Policy: The Gulf Crisis and Beyond," *Asian Survey* 32 (1992), p. 271.
10. United Nations Document S/PV.3117, pp. 4-5.
11. United Nations Document S/PV.3082, p. 10.
12. United Nations Press Release SC/6021, p. 11.
13. United Nations Document S/PV.3106, pp. 50-52.
14. United Nations Document S/PV.3191, p. 22.
15. United Nations Document S/PV.3522, p. 16.
16. United Nations Document S/PV.3063, p. 61.
17. United Nations Document S/PV.3413, p. 10.
18. United Nations Document S/PV.3392, p. 4.
19. United Nations Document S/PV.3217, pp. 33-34.
20. United Nations Document S/PV.3114, pp. 10-11.
21. United Nations Document S/PV.3262, p. 4.
22. United Nations Document S/PV.3470, p. 5.
23. Barbara Crossette, "U.N. Mission to Haiti Reprieved; Offer by Canada Overcomes Chinese," *New York Times,* 1 March, 1996.
24. United Nations Document S/PV.3143, p. 4.
25. United Nations Document S/PV.3212, pp. 42-43.
26. United Nations Document S/PV.3461, p. 7.
27. United Nations Document S/PV.3553, p. 12.
28. United Nations Document S/PV.3188, p. 22.
29. Inter Press Service, 13 August 1992.
30. United Nations Document S/PV.3376, p. 9.
31. United Nations Document S/PV.3430, p. 6.
32. United Nations Press Release SC/6143.
33. United Nations Document S/PV.2943, p. 51.

34. Susumu Awanohara, "Mutual Abstainers," *Far Eastern Economic Review*, 13 December, 1990, p. 10.
35. George Joffe, "The New Libyan Crisis," *Jane's International Review* 4, no. 6, p. 261.
36. Yitzhak Shichor, "China and the Role of the United Nations in the Middle East: Revised Policy," *Asian Survey* 31, (1991), p. 269.
37. Anne Penketh, "China holds up UN action on Cuba, Haiti," *Agence France Presse*, 27 February, 1996.

6

A JAPANESE VIEW ON RESTRUCTURING THE SECURITY COUNCIL

MASAYUKI TADOKORO

The United Nations is facing an identity crisis. During the Cold War the UN was largely paralyzed in its critical mission of collective security. The reason was widely believed to lie in the political confrontation between the two superpowers. Ironically, however, the dysfunction of the UN helped almost everyone to project onto it her or his own expectations about roles the UN should play. For idealistic cosmopolitans, the UN should be comparable to a world government, replacing states on the national level. For some internationalists, the UN was expected to be a body for collective security, which would institutionalize the exercise of force within the international framework. For traditional realists, the UN was an international forum where national governments play conventional diplomatic games. For developing countries, the UN is a place to express their dissatisfaction toward rich countries, to demand the redistribution of world wealth, and to offset their underrepresentation in the international political game. Needless to say, the UN was extensively used for political propaganda by both the United States and the Soviet Union, as well as by developing countries. Despite enormous differences, so long as the UN was not a functioning body the UN could enjoy almost everyone's high hopes.

The Necessity of Restructuring

The end of the Cold War and the brilliant victory of the multilateral forces in the Gulf War created a perception that the UN was finally freed from the paralysis caused by vetoes and the intractable ideological confrontation between the two superpowers, and that it was at long last beginning to do what it was born to do. The sharp increase in peacekeeping missions, and its success in Cambodia, seemed to endorse the optimism. After the disaster in Somalia and endless difficulties in the former Yugoslavia, however, the optimism rapidly yielded to disillusion and criticism of the UN. It is now clear that the roles the UN was expected to take required taking too heavy responsibilities upon itself, and that the future roles of the UN must be more carefully discussed and redefined.

Any restructuring of the Security Council must take into account the situation surrounding the UN. Although ongoing discussion on the issue, particularly in Japan, is focused on the expansion of the permanent membership and veto power, if restructuring is reduced merely to a game for stronger representation by some member countries, it may only satisfy the vanity of the new permanent member(s). The restructuring issue must be examined in relation to the future roles of the UN. Restructuring, in itself, cannot create a strong UN. But a better institutional framework would induce member states to work through the UN and inject more resources for UN activities. This chapter proposes four major changes:

1. Expand the role of the Security Council to social and economic fields,
2. Enlarge the Council's membership to a total of 20 to 25 states,
3. Give permanent membership to Japan, Germany, and several developing countries,
4. Introduce a weighted voting system to replace the current veto system, which would virtually protect the veto power of at least the existing permanent members.

This chapter discusses various future roles of the UN. It then examines four requirements which any restructuring must satisfy. Finally, it considers the implications of restructuring for Japan and that country's external policy.

The Limit of Collective Security and the Future Roles of the UN

According to the UN Charter, the Security Council is the only body whose decisions are binding on member states. The collective security mechanism envisioned in the Charter (Articles 42 to 46) provides that the Security Council will decide upon the use of force and calls on member states to contribute forces that would be commanded by the Military Staff Committee. This mechanism has never been activated and will not be activated in the foreseeable future. The reason for that is simply that international society is not developed enough to entrust the international body with such critical decision making concerning the use of military force.

In practice, enforcement actions under Chapter VII of the Charter have taken a far more ad hoc form. The Gulf War was fought by multilateral forces whose action was authorized by the Security Council. The peacekeeping operations in the former Yugoslavia and Somalia contained elements of enforcement actions, but were primarily developed from traditional peacekeeping operations. The ad hoc nature of these collective military actions will mark the limit of UN enforcement actions so long so the basic structure of the international system remains one consisting of enormously heterogeneous sovereign states.

In view of the current political mood in major member states, even these less systematic enforcement actions are unlikely to be repeated in the near future. Because of the overextension of UN activities after the Cold War, the UN's capability has become excessively degraded. Nevertheless, the UN still is the only global organization with a history of more than a half century. If multilateral military action is to be taken, the UN will often be the most legitimate and authoritative mechanism through which member countries can organize their concerted efforts.

The existence of a mechanism, however, certainly does not guarantee that the mechanism will be used by member states. Activation of collective military action depends essentially on the political will of major member states. Difficulties of undertaking collective security actions are well known. Particularly in the UN, where interests, power, and commitment differ greatly among the member countries, it is likely either that many irresponsible decisions will be made, or that no effective decisions will be taken. Thus, enforcement actions organized under the Security Council will not be a regular institutional process, but rather will be possible only under exceptional conditions, when the interests of major countries converge and the political will to run risks is shared among them.

The risks and costs involved in traditional peacekeeping operations are more limited because a working cease-fire is a precondition of launching a new mission. Nevertheless, a dramatic expansion in the number and mandate of peacekeeping operations after the Cold War has overstretched the UN to a dangerous level. While traditional troop contributors have provided well-trained contingents for peace missions, many complex recent operations have had to be run by undertrained and underequipped troops. These peacekeepers have had to deal with increasingly complicated and difficult intrastate conflicts, in which militia and armed civilians show little discipline and have ill-defined chains of command, rather than with interstate conflicts in which regular military forces of established states are the main actors. More support by member governments is obviously necessary for successful discharge of the missions. But the bleak record of financial contributions by the member states symbolizes the UN's failure to attract as much support as is necessary for the post–Cold War rapid increase in the number of peacekeeping operations.

A lesson from recent painful experiences is that member states must be more selective in launching missions through the UN.[1] The UN is not the only framework through which states can conduct peace missions. Members could use regional frameworks or bilateral frameworks. In some cases, they could intervene unilaterally. Nonintervention is also a conceivable choice, since intervention into civil conflicts could make things worse rather than better. In any case, as long as the UN can attract only limited support from its member states, it cannot deal with all conflicts in the world, and other frameworks could work better depending on the nature of conflicts.

Compared with other frameworks for intervention, the UN's comparative advantage lies in its impartiality and in its global character. Since the UN enjoys relative detachment from regional conflicts, it can work as a mechanism through which nonregional major powers can be brought onto the scene with less suspicion directed toward them. In cases in which countries in the region work in concert, a regional framework can be more effective than the UN. Thus the UN cannot be effective in every conflict all over the world, and should concentrate on the activities where it has a comparative advantage. Overstretch of the UN carries another danger. In view of the increasingly inward-looking attitudes of major countries, there is a real danger that the UN will be used as a dumping ground for impossible conflicts when major powers want to abandon responsibility. This would not only encourage isolationist attitudes in the major powers but would also severely damage the UN's authority.

While the UN's role in some fields should be limited below the inflated level attempted immediately after the Cold War, the Security Council must expand its roles in other areas. Since one of the major characteristics of many post–Cold War conflicts is a total breakdown of a national government rather than a struggle between firmly established states, the plight of failed states and a lack of any keen geostrategic interests there on the part of the superpowers after the Cold War prompted use of the UN to intervene into situations of previously unexperienced difficulty. So far the UN has been preoccupied with emergency relief and attempted containment of local struggles. But traditional peacekeeping and humanitarian activities can offer at best a short-term alleviation of the problems. To establish functioning elements of international governance, more long-term and wide-ranging efforts at peacebuilding will be required. Efforts in social and economic fields can be useful for preventive measures as well. For example, ethnic tension in developing countries can be eased by training of local police forces and judicial officers as well as preventive deployment of foreign troops. In addition, in view of the fact that economic sanctions are being widely used to contain a threat, a measure to rectify the disruptive impacts of sanctions on vulnerable third countries must be found. This also involves much economic effort.

Thus there should be a stronger emphasis on the link between the social and economic fields on the one hand, and the security agenda on the other. Failed states pose a serious direct threat to international security in the form of massive outflows of refugees. In addition, in a world in which international media show extraordinary disasters on television to people sitting in their living rooms, abandoning people experiencing massive suffering would cause a general degeneration of moral responsibility in international society. The Security Council must therefore expand its activities from strictly military and police activities to economic and social fields. It certainly does not follow that peacekeeping and possible enforcement actions should be ruled out. The Security Council, however, must be prepared for a new type of security threat arising from post–Cold War conditions.

Requirements for a Reformed Security Council

Mobilization of Resources for the United Nations

The UN can be a strong organization only when it can command adequate resources. It is well known that the existing composition of the Security Council does not reflect the distribution of economic power in today's world. The relative decline of importance of the permanent five members, for example, is well reflected in their contracting share in the UN budget. In 1948 their share of the regular budget amounted to around 70 percent. Since then it has dropped steadily, to a current level of about 42 percent. For the peacekeeping budget, the share of the permanent members is far larger, but the United States and Russia have failed to pay their assessments and actually have been the two largest violators of the financial obligation provided by the UN Charter. The remarkable economic growth of Germany and Japan, and the corresponding expansion of their financial contribution, is common knowledge. But other newly emerging economic powers, such as the Republic of Korea and other East Asian countries, should not be forgotten, and there should be a way to mobilize their resources.

Of course, resources essential to various UN roles are not confined to economic ones. Well-trained contingents for peacekeeping are important for UN activities, as is the capacity to provide humanitarian and emergency relief. In these respects also the direct contribution of the permanent members, particularly that of the two superpowers, was modest at least until the end of the Cold War.

In order for the UN to be an effective organization, it is logical to think that more closely involving member states with valuable resources in the decision making process is desirable so as to induce them to participate actively in the UN mission. At the same time, it must be remembered that resources necessary for the UN are limited in comparison to the scale of national economies of most member countries. Although the budget for peacekeeping in 1993 amounted to a record-high $3.5 billion, it was tiny (about 0.5 percent) compared to world gross military spending in that year. Although the U.S. Congress refused to pay the 31 percent American assessment for peacekeeping, its $1 billion contribution is nearly negligible by comparison with a U.S. defense budget of nearly $300 billion.

Thus what is really important is the political will for member states to dispense their resources vigorously for UN activities. The UN, therefore, has to be organized in such a way as to promote the willingness of member states to participate actively in the UN missions. For underrepresented rising powers, the UN can be an attractive forum in which to express themselves and to satisfy their national pride. In other words, newly rising powers should be given more representation in the Security Council since there is a chance that they would be more willing to inject new vitality to the UN, which, in turn, might stimulate greater contributions from established powers.

Efficiency

If effective action through mobilizing as many resources as possible were the only criterion, the conclusion on reform of the Security Council would be easy. The maximum involvement of member states would be the answer. But there is a contradictory need, which is the efficiency of the Security Council. For the Security Council to play a strong role in peacekeeping and crisis management, decisions must be made promptly without going through too cumbersome a procedure. Since the most common UN military role is peacekeeping rather than enforcement, timely and well-managed use of forces will be far more important than the scale of forces. It therefore is usually argued that the number of members must be kept small for the sake of efficient decision making.

Obviously there is a trade-off between legitimacy and efficiency of the Council, and a reasonable balance must be found. It certainly is not advisable to give many seats to miniature states. Nor would it be a good idea to expand the Council to the size of ECOSOC. However, the number of member states is by no means the only relevant factor in determining the efficiency of decision making, nor is it probably even the most important factor.

The IMF, for example, has worked reasonably efficiently when financial crises occur even though its Board of Executive Directors has as many as 20 seats, and the 15 members other than those from the U.S., Britain, France, Germany, and Japan are selected by their constituencies and exercise their voting power jointly. Efficiency is secured not by the small number of members, but by the fact that voting power is distributed in proportion to each country's quota in the Fund. Although this weighted voting system of the IMF provides a major source of dissatisfaction on the part of developing countries, it is inevitable that a country with heavier financial responsibility demands a larger say in the running of a financial institution.

In the realm of international security, it is difficult to measure the ability of a country to discharge its responsibilities. Nevertheless, it should be manageable to have 20 to 25 members in the Council although it should not be as large as ECOSOC with its 54 seats. What probably is far more important for efficiency of the Security Council is the degree of political leadership exerted by major powers. No matter how painful the process may be, it will not be impossible to convince other members if strong leadership is exerted by the major powers in the Council and an appropriate distribution of voting power is proposed. The critical question is not the number of the members but whether major powers such as the United States are prepared to invest as much political capital as is necessary for timely action. Unfortunately, no institutional reform can guarantee strong political leadership by major powers. But reform can facilitate that leadership. Thus, even after an expansion of the membership of the Security Council, negative effects on efficiency could be considerably offset by giving a stronger say to major powers.

Legitimacy

The Security Council and its permanent members are almost doomed to be subject to severe criticism from unrepresented developing countries. It is obviously an aristocratic body in which permanent members can exercise vetoes. For developing countries, a reform that entailed permanent membership for Germany and Japan only would make the Council too Northern and too European, with four permanent members from Europe. A more "democratic" Security Council, with more "equitable" geographical representation, will be necessary to satisfy the developing countries. Moreover, the permanent members have formed an exclusive club in which important issues are discussed in a closed informal setting. The formal open session of the Council has turned into a ritual in which the member countries express their official positions and follow official procedures to pass a resolution. A common complaint is that binding decisions are taken without active involvement of poor small countries. Thus, developing countries want a more "transparent" deliberation process in the Security Council.

Yet the notions of "democracy" and "equitable" representation in international organization are difficult to define. If they mean that all members should be treated in exactly equal fashion, that would give absolute importance to the status of sovereignty to an extent that would be inconsistent with the very existence of the international organization.

Would it be democratic to give the same say to China, with its over 1 billion population, as to Monaco? Or would it be democratic to give equal weight to small countries, whose assessment to the UN regular budget may be as small as 0.01 percent, as to the United States, whose assessment is 25 percent? With the enormous heterogeneity in the world, it is difficult to know what constitutes equality and fairness. Equitable geographical representation is also a difficult criterion to apply in practice. Regional powers are usually competitors (e.g., Argentina and Brazil) and sometimes even enemies (e.g., India and Pakistan). For all regional powers to be made permanent members would result in unmanageable inflation of the Security Council to the extent it would become totally inefficient.

Nevertheless, it is essential for the UN to be regarded as a legitimate organization. Since the UN does not have any autonomous source of power, its authority very much depends on its legitimacy. In addition, the unique value of the UN consists in its universal nature. The Security Council, therefore, must not be merely a forum for rich or powerful countries—like the G7 meeting—but instead needs to secure the political commitment of developing countries on global issues.

The veto power of the permanent members can be regarded as undemocratic by nonpermanent member states. During the Cold War, the veto was an important mechanism to secure the effectiveness of the Security Council. The resolutions of the Council, therefore, were relatively effective although resolutions were passed relatively infrequently, only when both the United States and the USSR agreed. Even after the Cold War, no matter what institutional rearrangement is made, no resolution can be effective unless major powers actively support it. Thus it is inevitable that major countries will be accorded some kind of veto power so as to enable the institution to function. Otherwise, major powers may abandon the UN and try to work through other frameworks such as the G7, or to act unilaterally. In such a case the world would lose its only universal organization.

Political Feasibility

It is one thing to envision a desirable arrangement of the Security Council. It is quite another to work out the measures needed to bring about the change. Any reform faces resistance from parties enjoying vested interests, and it requires political capital to invest in the process of change. Since a meaningful reform of the Security Council requires revision of the Charter, any formula that is not acceptable to existing permanent members will never materialize.

This implies an important condition for reform: there cannot be any attempt to downgrade existing permanent members in an explicit manner. And, as we have seen, one of the major goals of reform is to mobilize more resources for the UN by making the organization reflect the changed reality of distribution of power in international society. It then follows that both Germany and Japan must be more closely involved in the affairs of the Security Council. But it is unthinkable that France and the United Kingdom, whose relative importance in the world has declined over the last 50 years, would be willing to give up their seats in the Council for the sake of the rising powers. Nor is it even imaginable that China would give up its seat for the sake of Japan.

Thus, on one hand, we must give more representation to rising powers. On the other hand, we must protect the vested interest of existing permanent members. The Council should be kept small to be effective, but it should also include developing countries to be legitimate. Obviously, careful balancing of contradictory needs is required to work out a politically feasible formula for the reform.

There might be more than one way to deal with this need, but one possible way to strike the required balance would be to introduce a weighted voting system comparable to that adopted by the IMF. Voting power could be calculated from such indicators as population, assessment, contribution of contingents to peacekeeping, and voluntary financial contributions. And a high percentage of voting power could be set to adopt a resolution.[2] Three to five developing countries plus Germany and Japan could be given permanent seats while another 12 to 15 nonpermanent members could be selected by regional constituencies. Many of these nonpermanent members might exercise their voting power jointly.

A big advantage of a weighted voting system is that it would transform the all-or-nothing kind of voting power (one vote or no representation, regular vote or veto) of member states into a continuous value. It therefore would enlarge a scope of bargaining among member states. While this approach might complicate negotiation among members, there are the following merits.

For existing permanent members, this may be an attractive formula because they can in practice preserve their veto powers by selecting a convenient index and giving themselves appropriate weight when calculating voting power and/or by setting a high percentage for adopting resolutions. Particularly for the United Kingdom and France, this formula would allow their EU partners to be represented without giving up their own seats. Newly emerging powers like Germany and Japan might be satisfied with this formula because they are not given second-class permanent seats without a veto, even if their voting power may not be as large as a practical veto. Newly industrializing countries as well as regional powers in the South would be given more importance, depending on their commitments to the UN. That in turn could induce them to become more actively involved in UN efforts. For developing countries also, this may be viewed as a positive step forward because the veto power would be formally, if not practically, abolished. If this formula were coupled with a review of voting power every five or ten years, they could hope for more equal representation in the future.

Japan and the Security Council

Japan is the most likely candidate for new permanent membership. Its financial contribution to the UN regular budget will be 16.75 per cent in 1997, more than the combined contribution of the four permanent members other than the United States. Any new UN initiative, including launching a new peacekeeping mission, is practically impossible without Japan's support. Japan obviously has been a well-behaved member of the UN, and—with the notable possible exceptions of China and Korea[3]—it is difficult for states to object openly to Japan's bid for membership. Moreover, Japan is a rich source of development aid programs and it is already the largest donor of Official Development Assistance. If the reformed Security Council deals with social and economic problems as well, Japan's deeper involvement would be an indispensable condition.

Nevertheless, Japanese attitudes toward membership are ambivalent. On one hand there has been growing willingness for Japan to play more active international roles even in military security fields, particularly after the Gulf War. Despite Japan's $13 billion contribution at the time of the Gulf War, it was paralyzed by self-imposed prohibition over its military activities beyond its territory proper, and was humiliated rather than respected for its pacifist posture. Those who became keenly aware of the limitations of "checkbook diplomacy" are now calling for Japan to be a "normal state" with as few self-restraints over its military roles as have other major countries. Japan's Security Council permanent membership is for them a natural step forward as well as a means to promote the "normal state."

On the other hand, pacifist and isolationist sentiments remain strong.[4] Japan's low-key military policy coupled with active pursuit of economic growth after World War II has been so successful that even many conservatives actually belong to the pacifist camp. Since inward-looking attitudes are widespread all over the world these days, it is not surprising that Japan has its own share. However, in Japan's case, isolationist sentiment is connected with an idealistic pacifist perspective denying the legitimacy of any military exercise, even one conducted through the UN.

Under such circumstances, it is hardly surprising that there were frictions between the Ministry of Foreign Affairs, which wants to boost Japan's prestige in the UN, and the recent cabinet headed by a Socialist, whose party kept claiming that the Self-Defense Forces were unconstitutional, and which obstinately objected to the SDF's dispatch to the peacekeeping mission in Cambodia. Despite the differences, there is a strong consensus in Japan that Japan's primary role in the UN is not military, but social and economic. Whereas the extreme pacifist view concerning military power is inconsistent not only with Japan's permanent membership in the Security Council but more widely in the UN itself, Japan's active involvement in the Security Council should not be viewed only from its role in traditional military and security fields. If the Security Council is to expand its activities into social and economic fields as this chapter proposes, there is a great deal Japan can offer. From a political viewpoint, stronger emphasis on the link between social and economic affairs on one hand and the security agenda on the other can work as a kind of quid pro quo for support of Japan's permanent membership by developing countries, which always complain about rich members' neglect of such matters.

In fact, an inactive Japan can be a more serious danger to the world than an imperialistic Japan. Japan's permanent membership would be important not for its limited symbolic dispatch of SDF contingents, but because it would induce Japan to be more active in international affairs. The pacifist element in Japan's foreign policy is very much a product of its postwar historical conditions. Japan was completely defeated in World War II, and the UN was originally an alliance against Germany and Japan. A peaceful or passive Japan was what the United States wanted until the Cold War started. Japan's neighbors have been skeptical about an active Japan for fear of the revival of an imperialist Japan.

For the Japanese themselves, a passive Japan was convenient because it did not need to waste its limited economic and political resources on involvement in power politics. This, however, certainly ceased to be an appropriate attitude for the second largest economy in the world.

The UN offers a workable and effective framework for Japan to become more active in the pursuit of its foreign policy because the biggest obstacle to an active Japan is its "legitimacy deficit," both externally and internally. The UN can legitimize Japan's active roles in global and regional affairs by more closely involving Japan into its decision-making process. This aspect is all the more important because of suppressed nationalism in Japan. Because of the "legitimacy deficit," Japanese nationalism has not been able to find Japan's proper role in the world and Japanese nationalism has tended to take the form of isolationist and pacifist anti-Americanism. Given the rising confidence of postwar generations of Japanese, it is both wasteful and somewhat dangerous to keep the Japanese mentality inward looking.

The same situation may apply to Germany. Its active role in international security affairs may generate skeptical reactions from neighboring countries. Nevertheless, Germany has multilateral frameworks such as NATO and the EU to institutionalize its roles. Since there is no comparable regional framework in Asia, the UN is particularly valuable for Japan. The UN can play an effective role in guiding the energy of Japan's rising new nationalism into a constructive direction by satisfying Japan's national pride and offering an international framework acceptable to former victims of Japan's prewar imperialism.

A Time to Change

Experiences after the Cold War amply showed us that it is still premature to expect systematic collective enforcement operations commanded by the UN. The UN lacks resources and infrastructure, and above all support from member states for ambitious but politically controversial operations. Thus, in the foreseeable future, there is no chance for collective security to function as it was pictured in the Charter. The UN will remain a mechanism selectively used by member countries. It will be effective principally as a forum to coordinate resources and political action by member states. No restructuring can guarantee the effectiveness of UN activities. Whatever reform is agreed upon, institutional rearrangement by itself cannot bring about a stronger UN. It is a dangerous illusion to assume that an institutional arrangement automatically will change the pattern of behavior of member states. It can only facilitate members' ability to work out agreements and to act in concert by offering a mechanism for consultation and bargaining.

Nevertheless, it is also true that member states need a stronger UN to promote a stable international environment. Since there are now so many players and issues in an increasingly fragile world, international institutions are indispensable to maintain an acceptable international order. Despite strong disillusion in recent years, the UN still provides the greatest hope for world order. The UN has unique assets. It has existed as the only universal organization dealing with many global issues. Conventions and practices accumulated over the last 50 years represent an incomparable asset. No matter how unsatisfactory the UN may be, it would be extremely difficult, and probably not even possible, to replace the UN with a brand new framework. The right question to be asked, therefore, is what sort of institutional arrangement can best strengthen the UN by promoting support by member states.

In view of the declining power and willingness of the permanent members to discharge their international responsibilities, it is essential to revitalize the UN by injecting new blood. Thus it is necessary to involve both Germany and Japan in the Security Council—but such a step is not enough. There should be a mechanism to mobilize resources of other and future rising powers. It is also necessary to induce countries with higher status to take more responsibility. A weighted voting system, connecting status with responsibility, is a way to meet the need. The Security Council can enjoy authority only when it is legitimate in the eyes of poor countries. It therefore should deal with social and economic issues that are as pressing problems for poor countries as are conventional military conflicts.

The momentum for restructuring seems to be rapidly dwindling, and may have been reduced to finding a way to get Japan and Germany onto the Security Council as permanent members. But while political mood changes over time, institutions long remain the same. The world will need a stronger UN in the future. Despite the highly pessimistic political mood surrounding the UN now, the present opportunity for change should be utilized so as to meet the long-term needs of the Organization.

NOTES

1. In his "Supplement to *An Agenda for Peace*," Boutros Boutros-Ghali admitted that the enforcement mission proposed in his original *An Agenda for Peace* was overly ambitious and practically gave up the idea of the peace enforcement units that he had put forth earlier. See *An Agenda for Peace,* 2nd ed. (New York: United Nations, 1995).
2. For example, in the IMF 85 percent of all votes are required to make decisions on important matters. The necessary threshold was raised in 1969 from 80 percent in order to preserve the veto power of the United States, whose quota had shrunk.
3. See Chi Young Park, "Korea and the United Nations: The First Fifty Years," *Korea and World Affairs* 19, (1995), pp. 612-31, 627-28: "There are still states that oppose the idea of including the so-called enemy states as permanent members with veto power. On this issue, South Korea has endorsed the idea of increasing the number of permanent members, but the newly-added permanent members should be without veto power."
4. See "Gaiko Ni Kansuru Seronchosa" (A Public Opinion Pool on Foreign Policy), Prime Minister's Office, October 1994, pp. 11-14.

7

SECURITY COUNCIL REFORM: INFORMAL MEMBERSHIP AND PRACTICE

IAN HURD

The most important parameters of the Security Council are fixed by the language of the Charter. These include the voting rules, the number of members, and the number, privileges, and identity of the permanent members. Like any good constitutional document, the Charter sets out clearly and definitively the basic structure of the governmental organs in question, and gives them a useful permanence. The trade-off for this clarity and permanence is an entrenchment of the status quo and a presumption against change, innovation, and reform. This creates a typical tension in constitutions between the need for evolution and interpretation as circumstances change, and the fundamental task of *constituting* the elemental rules of the game. In the case of the Charter, as the constitution of the United Nations including the Security Council, we see perhaps the worst of both worlds: the amendment formula is extremely stringent so that formal structures are almost cast in stone, and the system in which the Organization operates is highly complex, dynamic, and volatile. It is unsurprising therefore that in the course of 50 years the formal, fixed shape of the Security Council should at times seem ill-matched to the flowing and changing patterns in the international system. And yet the Security Council has maintained some relevance over this period. Despite being reconstituted only once, by the relatively slight alteration of adding four nonpermanent seats in 1965, it has not been abandoned as anachronistic.

This chapter suggests that some basic insights from the theory of organizations can help us understand how the Security Council has survived the dramatic shifts of the international system since 1945. In that time, the particulars of the international system have changed greatly, through processes that include decolonization, the Cold War, and the breakup of the Soviet Union (to name but a few), but the formal composition of the Security Council has scarcely been altered. The "open systems" perspective borrowed from organization theory encourages us to look at how an organization adapts to change in its environment. An open system is one that relies significantly on its environment for supplies, markets, or legitimacy, and that must make internal changes to accommodate developments in the environment. When studying these internal changes, it is useful to distinguish between changes in the *formal* as opposed to the *informal* structure: the first involves official reconfiguration of the structure of the organization; the second involves change in the practices or routines of the body without formal restructuring. That only one formal change to the structure of the Security Council has been made to date suggests the Council's "coping mechanism" for environmental change has been more in the area of informal practice than in official structural reform.[1]

This chapter will not review all the procedural and consultative practices of the Security Council since 1945.[2] Instead, it will present the case that an organization's informal structure must be taken seriously, and suggest that the institutionalized practice of consultation between Security Council members and states not on the Council constitutes a significant development in the informal structure of the Council, one driven by the major shifts in the international environment. Two sets of states have particularly interesting consultative access to Security Council deliberations, the states of the Non-Aligned Movement, and the states that contribute troops and material to peacekeeping operations. In both these cases states without a seat on the Security Council (either permanent or nonpermanent) may enjoy a kind of de facto membership by virtue of their informal consultations with members. Also worth investigating is the degree of informal access enjoyed by Japan and Germany, as the largest states without permanent representation on the Council.

One aim of this chapter is to counter the assertion, common in proposals for UN reform in the 1990s, that the Security Council is ineffective *because* key states are not represented with permanent seats. The implication of this assertion is that permanent membership on the Security Council should be redistributed or increased to reflect the new distribution of power in the international system. While there may be good reasons for reconstituting the Council, the terms of this assertion do not necessarily follow. The chapter is organized to challenge each of these terms in turn. First, it will be argued that external change need not reduce the Council's effectiveness even in the absence of formal change, as long as the informal practice of the Council adapts to the new environment. Students of organizations in other fields have generated a body of research documenting the development and consequences of informal structures. These grow up parallel to formal structures, and can in some cases contribute significantly to the pursuit of the organization's official goals. In the case of the Security Council, the relevant change in the external environment is movement in the relative weight of the great powers since 1945. The set of four or five largest powers, which is what the permanent membership was originally intended to reflect, has shifted since the UN Security Council was first cast and this has generated stresses for the Council. The corresponding kind of adaptation we might expect would be a change in the membership of the body, but it might be informal rather than formal.

The second section examines the history of changes to the composition of the Security Council. That history includes one formal change and a steady stream of modifications to the informal practices of the body. For the purposes of determining the Council's "effective membership," significant informal structures may be found in the pattern of consultation and opinion-taking outside the formal membership. In the extreme, this consultation may reach the point where some states may have informal membership and even an informal veto in the Council. By "informal membership" I mean a state that is not a member of the Council but that is consulted by Council members, particularly by one or more of the permanent five, in advance of significant decisions. For this to constitute an effective voice, the consulters must take seriously the opinions and objections of the nonmember state. By "informal veto" I mean the capacity that such states might have to prevent decisions from being taken. This sense of the phrase informal veto is different than that used to refer to the potential blocking power of the non-aligned members on the Council. Given these definitions, the notions in this chapter obviously refer to only a small number of states, or to several states on only a few issue areas, but their relation to the Council is significant.

The term "informal consultation" is often used in a different sense to refer to the consultation that takes place *among* Security Council members in advance of a formal meeting or decision of the Council. These consultations, and the resulting increase in unanimous decisions of the Council, have increased significantly since the late 1970s and have changed the dynamic of the Council in important ways.[3] In the present chapter, however, I concentrate on the less-studied consultation between Security Council members and nonmembers. The effect of nonmembers on Council deliberations is an intriguing example of organizational response to external sources of power. Because of the structure of power within the Council, this will mostly relate to consultation by the permanent members with nonmembers. However, it is also worth investigating the patterns of consultation between nonpermanent members and nonmembers, particularly within the Non-Aligned Movement.

Recognizing the practice of informal membership on the Council has several interesting implications, explored in the third section. First, it contributes to an understanding of how the Council has maintained its effectiveness despite the enormous changes in the international political environment and the difficulty of formal change, and as such it shows how it may survive in the future if reform proves impossible in the present round of discussions. Informal membership has in the past taken some pressure away from the drive to restructure the Council formally, and could plausibly continue to do so. Second, it provides an indication about what kinds of modifications the existing Council members have found essential to the effective operation of the body, and thus may be a guide to which states and which forms of power should be included in a restructured Council. Finally, it suggests that if formal Council membership is indeed a desired goal for the major member-states not presently on the Council, it is likely for reasons other than the effective power over outcomes that membership confers—symbolic reasons, perhaps playing out in domestic politics, may well lie at the heart of the matter.

The concluding section reverses course somewhat and points to some reasons why we might indeed value formal change in Security Council membership. The drive to win membership on the Council may, as just mentioned, be motivated by the symbolic rather than practical effects of participation and membership. The Security Council is a prominent body with restricted membership, and as a result a high prestige is attached to membership. The symbolic rewards to membership should not be discounted in discussions of reform, and may in themselves be sufficient reason to attempt to change the formal composition of the Council. Further, expanded or recast formal membership may give the Security Council new legitimacy to take action where previously it could not. Adding new members, particularly permanent members, will add to the resources at the Council's disposal, and may enable new and worthwhile action. The fact that there may be some such reasons in favor of formal change suggests in conclusion that those who promote membership reform must be clear about their reasons for doing so, and that they cannot base that argument on the simple assertion of Council ineffectiveness. Thus this chapter does not present an argument against all formal restructuring of the body, only for correctly specifying the reasons why an altered membership might be wanted.

Organizations as Open Systems

A basic image in organization theory is that of the organization as "open system." This encompasses a variety of theoretical approaches that share a common concern with the ways in which an organization's environment influences and challenges its structures and practices. The environment is composed, depending on the object of study, of other organizations, public bureaus and regulators, community or social groups, labor-training organizations, and the like. Each of these elements influences the work of the organization itself, probably both positively and negatively. "To embrace the notion of organizations as open systems is to acknowledge that organizations are penetrated by their environments in ways that blur and confound any simple criterion for distinguishing the one from the other."[4] External actors and forces have an effect on the internal structure and processes of an organization, and for the most part it is the organization that must adapt to or insulate itself from the environment (rather than the organization being able to control its environment).[5] One branch of the open systems approach concentrates on the fact that the environment may provide resources that the organization requires, such as markets, supplies, or legitimacy, while another branch is interested in how change in the environment induces change (or simply the need for change) in the organization.

Organizations need certain resources in order to function: firms need markets, suppliers, personnel; public agencies need funding, legitimization, perhaps markets. Uncertainty in the supply of these resources is a source of stress for the organization, and so there will be a constant search for the correct balance at each moment between internalizing and externalizing these sources. This idea has been developed as the "resource dependency" approach to organizations.[6] The paradigm case of the resource dependency approach is the manufacturing firm that aims to reduce uncertainty in supply and demand by expanding itself "forward" into the business of marketing and distribution, and "backward" into the processing of raw materials.[7] The environment of most organizations is constantly changing, and the organization's leaders must have some sense for how to cope with this change. Environmental change might present new opportunities, such as expanding markets or a supply of highly skilled labor, or new demands, such as regulatory pressures or shrinking markets. However, it is generally not known (or knowable) in advance whether a change is positive or negative; change is simply change. Failure to adapt sufficiently to the new conditions may mean the obsolescence of the organization, and bankruptcy for a firm or its equivalent for a public agency. Evolutionary analogies are commonly used in discussions of these processes of "environmental selection."

Organizational adaptation might take one of two forms: formal restructuring or informal reshaping. A living organization is a combination of formal structure and informal practice. The former is composed of the pieces of the organization chart: lines of authority, bureaucratic positions, fixed hierarchical relations, and the formal competencies of offices. The components of informal practice are harder to identify or measure, but are arguably at least as important.[8] These are the actual patterns of communication, interpersonal relations, ties to outside groups, and relations of power. It seems likely that informal practice will always be worth investigating because, on the one hand, the formal rules cannot specify every contingency, and on the other, human creativity seems to be naturally inclined to subvert formal procedure. Informal change may be at least as effective as formal change, as the former responds functionally to the immediate needs of participants rather than tending to be centralized, rationalized, and imposed from above. Where formal restructuring is ruled out or for some other reason is impossible, the entire pressure for adaptation falls on informal practice and the organization may change drastically. Nevertheless, formal structure places limits on the direction and extent of informal evolution, which can be measured in the degree to which leaders are sticklers for following procedures and for operating "by the book."

From the point of view of an organization theorist, the Security Council is a classic example of an open system. It is both highly sensitive to its environment and highly dependent on it. The environment in this case is the sum of the international political, military, and economic systems, which include all the states, individuals, refugee floods, and other forces that create the "threats to the international peace and security" with which the Security Council must be concerned. The Security Council relies on its environment both for the various crises it is responsible for managing and for the resources it must mobilize to perform those tasks. In addition, the Council is literally composed of elements of its environment in that its members are also state participants in these systems. This is an extreme example of the blurring of organization and environment that is characteristic of an open system. To remain effective in such a setting, the Security Council must be responsive to changes in the international system, both to maintain the ability to mobilize states and other actors and also to monitor impending international crises. The particular external change we are interested in is the shifting relative power positions of states, making the case that an internal change in Council membership is presumably needed. How has the Council coped to date with these massive changes in its environment?

Change in the Security Council

It is clear that the composition of the Security Council no longer reflects the actual distribution of power in the international system. Since the permanent membership was first cast in 1945, the continuing dynamic of international political and economic development has raised some nonmember states higher than many members, and has eroded the base of capabilities of some permanent members. Perhaps the most stark example is that Japan, without a seat on the Council, now has an assessed contribution to the UN regular budget that exceeds the combined assessments for four of the five permanent members. Change has also occurred in some people's view of what the metric should be for inclusion in the "Great Power club":[9] the relationship between economic and military strength is no longer clear; some suggest the permanent members should reflect more of global diversity, which originally was thought satisfied by the distribution of nonpermanent seats; and several other properties of states, ranging from size of population to contributions to peacekeeping to promptness of paying dues, may now qualify as criteria for inclusion. Precisely which set of states now constitutes the great powers, worthy of a permanent seat, is now more difficult to specify or to defend than in 1945. These changes have had the result of leaving some of the most important states in the system without formal representation on the Council. Following the resource-dependency approach to organizations outlined above, we should expect to see the Council react by attempting to bring within its ambit those states that can supply the financial, military, or legitimating goods of value to the Council.

The incorporation of these states might take place through formal change of Council membership or informal change of Council procedures. However, the latter is much more easily accomplished than the former. Under Articles 28-32, the Security Council is the master of its own practices and procedures. Even to the extent that its procedures are codified, as in the *Repertoire of the Practice of the Security Council*, they can be altered by the Council as needed. Several authors have described the development within the Council of new procedures for consultation among informal groups of members, and between members and outside parties.[10] Only a small number of important questions of a constitutional nature are fixed by outside authority, such as by the Charter or the UN membership as a whole, for which change would require outside approval or ratification. These questions include the number of Security Council seats and their allocation between permanent and nonpermanent members, and the voting majorities needed for different types of questions. Alteration of these variables must follow the procedure from Article 108, which sets a compound standard for revision, requiring two-thirds approval in the General Assembly, and ratification by two-thirds of UN members, including the five permanent members of the Security Council. Since formal change of membership is clearly more difficult than the informal inclusion of states, we would expect the Council to proceed as much as possible by modifications to its procedures and practices.

Formal Change in Membership

Unlike the League Covenant, the Charter contains no provision for changing the number of permanent Council seats or of members generally, other than the standard Charter revision formula. The Charter does allow that nonmembers may be invited to participate in matters that directly relate to their interests, and under Article 44 these nonmembers may even be allowed to vote, although this last provision has never been used.[11]

The history of formal change in Security Council membership is short. One Charter revision has been accomplished with respect to Security Council membership in the history of the organization. In 1963, after several years of fast growth in UN membership and consequent diminution of the relative size of the Council, the newly independent states succeeded in amassing enough support for a Charter amendment to increase from six to ten the number of nonpermanent seats, and from seven to nine the number of votes required to pass a resolution.[12] A corresponding change was needed in the distribution of seats among regional groups, and this was achieved by a General Assembly resolution in December 1963.

The increase in nonpermanent membership went a short distance to remedying the underrepresentation of small and medium states, in terms of both numbers and voting power, but it was an extremely conservative change. The enlarged Council still comprised a smaller proportion of UN members than it had in 1945, and made no change in the composition or privileges of the permanent membership. The conservatism of the amendment, and the fact that still today this represents the single formal change in the shape of the Security Council since 1945, should prompt us to explore the informal ways the Council has accommodated environmental change.

Informal Change in Membership

Informal consultation with nonmembers of the Council has developed into a significant operating strategy for the permanent members of the Security Council, and in the terms of organization theory this has blurred the practical distinction between member and nonmember, between organization and environment. It may also have blunted the enthusiasm of nonmembers for changing the composition of the Council, or even its basic principles of operation. The increase in informal participation by nonmembers has been driven in large part by changes in the international system, for instance as non-Council members have taken on responsibility for supplying peacekeeping operations and as small, independent-minded states have come to dominate the General Assembly.

Several states or groups of states are effectively included in some Security Council deliberations despite not having either permanent or nonpermanent membership. This informal inclusion has helped the

Council remain more effective than it would otherwise have been as the international system has departed from the image of 1945. Which states are included depends in part on the issue at hand. As a general matter, Germany and Japan are consulted by the Western three permanent members on most important issues even when these two are not occupying nonpermanent seats. This is due to the now-dominating economic positions of these two states. The importance of consultation was underlined by the coalitional politics of the Gulf War, where the United States was widely seen as taking all the important decisions on its own and only afterwards soliciting support and financing from its putative "partners."[13] With this experience as the backdrop, Germany and Japan, among others, have pressed for more active consultations with the Security Council permanent members in advance of decision making.

Other nonmembers of the Security Council are included only on specific issues, or by more specific devices. These include Israel, whose special relationship with the United States gives it access to Council information and an effective voice in opposition when needed, the states of the Non-Aligned Movement (NAM), and, more recently, the countries that contribute troops or materials to peacekeeping operations. It is worth examining in more detail the last two of these groups.

The case of the non-aligned states is relatively straightforward, and shows how a change in the system has prompted both formal and informal change in the shape and practice of the organization. The group was founded in 1961 but it is really since the late 1970s that its collective identity has been felt in the Security Council, due to improvement in its organization and a more activist approach. The cohesion and common interests of the NAM group has declined in most other fora due to the diversity of its members, but for the purposes of the United Nations they remain relatively united. NAM members generally have common interests in seeing limits placed on the powers of the Security Council and of the permanent five in particular, and in increasing opportunities for voice by smaller members. With the non-aligned states holding an ever increasing share of votes in the General Assembly, their collective capacity to obstruct, delegitimize, and otherwise complicate the operation of the Security Council has increased, and in response the permanent five have had to increase their sensitivity to NAM views in the Council. Even though none of their number has a permanent seat, the NAM always have representation on the Security Council because their numerical dominance in the General Assembly assures a steady stream of elections to temporary seats and a bloc of between five and eight on the Council. In addition, although for reasons of its own and to mixed reaction, China has often taken it upon itself to "represent" the non-aligned view within the permanent five; in 1992, China also gained observer status at NAM conferences.

There are many interesting aspects to the non-aligned influence on Security Council affairs,[14] but what we are interested in here is how the NAM as a group provides access to Security Council business for states that are neither permanent nor nonpermanent members of the Council. This takes the form of regular consultations, before and after Council meetings, between NAM Council members and NAM states not on the Council, usually organized according to the regional groupings by which nonpermanent members are selected. The effectiveness of NAM "pre-meeting" consultations beginning in the late 1970s was a spur to other Council members, particularly permanent members, to begin their own informal conversations among each other, and with outside states.

The desired effect of consultations for the non-aligned state in the Council is to increase the normative force of its vote and opinions by having them stand for the views of many others outside the body. Relegated by the voting rules to a marginal status, a nonpermanent member must be sensitive to such bonuses in its potential power. A former Indian representative on the Council has written that "The usefulness and the standing of non-permanent members depend mainly on the attitude of cooperation, understanding, and discussion they adopt in relation to the delegations outside the Council."[15] For the state not on the Council at all, the purpose of these consultations is to overcome the exclusion from formal membership and find a way to have at least a minor voice in its proceedings. Because the consultations among the NAM center around nonpermanent rather than permanent members, their ultimate effect on Council action is limited in the main to matters of procedure and timing.[16] The NAM representatives on the Council do not have the voting power to block proposed action or to mobilize inaction into action; the "NAM veto" requires such a high degree of NAM consensus that it is not often a credible threat, and has rarely been decisive in blocking a resolution.

Because of the power dynamics in the Council, informal consultations that involve the permanent members with nonmembers should have a more substantive effect. This appears to be true of the recently institutionalized practice of consultations between the Council and the states that contribute personnel or materials to peacekeeping operations (generically known as "troop-contributing countries" or TCCs). This new institution is a clear example of successful "lobbying" by a class of nonmembers for more participation in Council deliberations on questions where their interests are potentially at stake. An "accountability gap" had emerged around peacekeeping contributions due to the fact that the framers of the Charter envisioned the permanent five being the principal providers to security operations, while most such operations have in fact been undertaken through the unanticipated device of "peacekeeping" with material contributions drawn mainly from the ranks of the medium and small states. Article 44 of the Charter provides for representation in the relevant Security Council deliberations for nonmember states that provide military forces for a Chapter VII enforcement action, and such participation is at the discretion of the contributing state, not the Council. It was not expected that this clause would prove significant since the main contributing states were expected to be the great powers, which were already endowed with permanent membership on the Council. However, contributors to peacekeeping operations, because of the status of peacekeeping as a creative interpretation of the Charter, do not fall under Article 44 and have no formal status in the Security Council. Just as peacekeeping itself was a flexible response to changing external and internal circumstances, the Security Council has had to adapt to the unexpected situation of having the majority of its resources provided voluntarily by states with no representation. In recent years this has proved a significant difficulty as the Secretary-General and the Security Council have sought increased contributions and extended mandates from states without a voice in the Council. The issue has become especially salient in the design and redesign of mission mandates, where the Council may be deciding to place troops in more serious peril than that for which they were originally contributed.

Troop-contributing countries have in the past lobbied for an institutionalized relationship with the Security Council, and their cause was recently taken up by the General Assembly's Special Committee on Peacekeeping Operations. The result is a set of new practices, codified in official statements of the President of the Security Council. An important Presidential statement of May 1994 standardized the regular monthly meetings between the Council President and representatives of troop-contributing countries, and noted with approval the growing practice of ad hoc trilateral meetings between the Secretariat, troop-contributing states, and interested Security Council members.[17] These meetings allow information to flow from the Council to the TCCs on the progress of missions, and allow the TCCs to make known to the

Council their opinions and objections on the operational uses of their personnel and materials.

The relations between the Council and the NAM on one hand, and the TCCs on the other, show how the Security Council has had to adapt itself to a changing international environment, creating institutional links to important nonmembers in order to accommodate circumstances not envisioned at the drafting of the Charter. As peacekeeping has become a primary vehicle for the Council to take action on international peace and security, the personnel needed to make peacekeeping work have not come mostly from within the Council, as the Charter expected, but from without. Following a resource-dependency approach, we would expect significant effort on the part of the "leaders" in the Council (i.e., the permanent members) to find a way to incorporate the holders of these resources within the parameters of the body. In the case of the NAM, the relevant environmental change is the growth in UN membership during the period of decolonization. This motivated one Charter revision, taking effect in 1965, and has changed the dynamic of the Council as well as the General Assembly.

These illustrative examples are not conclusive evidence for the hypothesis that informal consultation with nonmembers of the Council can substitute for formal membership changes. Detailed empirical research of communications patterns and nonmembers' opinions would be needed to make that case definitively. Further research would also be worthwhile into the significant cases of Germany and Japan—the importance of these two states to the international system, and their capacity to "make or break" many proposed Security Council actions, suggest their preferences would be extensively polled by the permanent five, and that among the nonmembers their "informal vetoes" may be the strongest. These cases would repay at a profit close empirical study. For the present purposes, however, having set out the framework for thinking about changes in the informal practice of the Security Council and provided some evidence that this does in fact matter, I only wish to show that several interesting and important implications might come from this future examination.

Implications

The practice of informal consultation is important for discussions of the membership of the Security Council in at least three ways. First, we should be attentive to the fact that if formal restructuring is really to be pursued, those states that are already included in Security Council practice by informal consultation are probably the prime candidates for formal inclusion in an expanded Council. Informal inclusion says something about the kinds of power found to be important in executing Security Council decisions. We can infer that states with "informal membership" provide some resource (likely financial, military, or legitimizing), that the Security Council needs and that this provided the basis for their informal inclusion in the first place.

A second implication is that any new Security Council structure should avoid institutionalizing the kind of permanent privilege that would become debilitating in the future. In line with the above analysis, what matters for an organization is its flexibility to meet shifts in its environment. This flexibility might be in formal structure or, more likely, in informal structure. In a multipolar international system, where centers of power are not clear, an international organization with the ambitions of the United Nations must be flexible enough to recognize that different groups of states will need to be incorporated on different issue areas. Membership should be somehow open-ended. A Security Council that consults widely outside its formal membership will be able to capitalize on the strengths of particular nonmembers as needed, without entrenching the higher decision costs that would come from taking them all on as permanent members. This is well illustrated by the pattern of relations between the Council and troop-contributing countries.

Third, to the extent that a nonmember state that is already heavily consulted on matters in its interests still presses for formal membership, we should recognize that membership is likely valued for its *symbolic* rather than *substantive* properties. Like membership in the Group of Seven, a Security Council seat is a scarce international resource that confers immense status. In this respect, it may be important for domestic reasons that a government be able to show its formal inclusion in such an important international forum. Japan and Germany stand out as examples of this phenomenon, although with some countervailing factors.[18] Equally, it may be important for existing Security Council members that, for instance, Japan or Russia not be denied this source of domestic legitimacy, if such a denial fuels domestic instability or revisionism. In either case, merely being able to say that a state is *consulted* sufficiently so that it has effective power close to that of a formal member is not enough. The same story could be told with respect to German membership. This approach says that Security Council membership is a symbolic, not functional, source of power, and it points to the difference between *membership* in the Council and *participation* in its decisions.[19] This distinction should be made by any model that emphasizes the degree to which a nonmember state is, in O'Neill's terms from chapter four, "satisfied" with the substantive outcomes of Council decisions—while clearly an important consideration in other circumstances, satisfaction with outcomes may not be the primary motivation for many of the states pressing for permanent membership. By no means should symbolic reasons be discounted in considering Security Council reform: symbols in politics are at least as important as material factors.

None of this should be read as minimizing the influence of formal Council membership. Indeed, a seat, either permanent or temporary, is a significant thing. Consider the power held by tiny Yemen in the Gulf War debates by virtue of being a temporary member at the time of the crisis. This power gave it potential leverage to extract concessions from the West, but also brought uncomfortable attention to the Yemeni position. As for permanent members, consider China's maneuvering in the Council discussion of replacing US troops in Haiti with a United Nations force in 1995. One report has it that "Bent on punishing Haiti for maintaining relations with Taiwan, Beijing demanded that the Security Council reduce the proposed 1,900-member commitment to 1,200." Further, "China also managed to cut the term of the deployment to four months from six and stipulated that it not be extended further."[20] Many similar examples emerge in Thalakada's chapter, illustrating the broad power possessed by a veto holder.

We should not jump automatically to formal revision of Security Council membership as the first reaction to changes in the distribution of international power. Where formal reform is ruled out, the evolution of informal practice may be an effective bridge between organizational structure and new external circumstances, prolonging the stability of what otherwise would be an anachronistic structure. Further, it is not clear that formal inclusion is necessarily better than informal inclusion. Indeed, a recast formal membership would raise the same problems of inertia and resistance to change that are at present bedeviling attempts to reconcile the structure of the Council with the new distribution of power in the system.

This is not to say there is no good reason for attempting formal revision, only that we must carefully separate real reasons from apparent reasons. It is worth looking briefly at some of the real reasons. First, as just noted, formal membership on the Council may be an important source of domestic legitimacy for the government involved. Second, this discussion has proceeded on the assumption that permanent membership is mostly about *stopping* action from being taken. However, it is possible that the opposite may be true, so that a reformed Council membership might allow the Council to *initiate* action on problems that at present are beyond the body's capacity or legitimacy. This is the key to calls, such as Tadokoro's, to include Germany and Japan as a means to increase their military or financial contributions. We could also imagine a case in which the Security Council could not act on a given regional crisis because the formal absence of a regional representative denied it the necessary legitimacy. To the extent that this is true, basing future reform on past and present practice will be unnecessarily conservative. In this sense, the full potential of the organization may not yet have been seen, and will not be seen unless the body is refashioned to include these actors.

In sum, it is clear that the United Nations is not operating at the level of effectiveness necessary to achieve the high ambitions set out in the Charter. However, it is not obvious that this discrepancy results from the fact that the five permanent members of the Security Council no longer include the five most important global powers. There is reason to believe from models of organizations in other settings that substantial effectiveness can be maintained even in the face of significant environmental change. The key is the flexibility and adaptiveness of the practices of the organization. Thus, while there may be good reasons for reallocating Security Council seats, they might have less to do with organizational effectiveness and more with the symbolic power of membership.

NOTES

1. Attention to the shifting practices of the United Nations, as opposed to its formal structure, appears to be increasing. See, for instance, Carolyn L. Willson "Changing the Charter: The United Nations Prepares for the Twenty-First Century," *American Journal of International Law* 90 (1996), pp.115-126, and Frederic L. Kirgis, Jr., "The Security Council's First Fifty Years," *American Journal of International Law* 89 (1995), pp. 506-39.
2. The formal catalogue of the Security Council's procedural rules is the ever provisional *Repertoire of the Practice of the Security Council, 1946 - 51* (New York: United Nations, Department of Political and Security Council Affairs,

1954) and its *Supplements*. The history of this compendium proves the dictum "C'est seul le provisoire qui dure."

3. See for instance, Sidney D. Bailey "The Evolution of the Practice of the Security Council," in Davidson Nicol, ed., *Paths to Peace: The UN Security Council and its Presidency*, (New York: Pergamon Press, 1981).
4. W. Richard Scott, *Organizations: Rational, Natural, and Open Systems*, 3rd ed. (Englewood, N.J.: Prentice-Hall, 1992), p. 181.
5. The opposite case, where organizational control of the environment is significant, may be evident in some circumstances. For arguments in this direction, see Charles Perrow, *Complex Organizations: A Critical Essay*, 3rd ed. (New York: McGraw-Hill, 1986).
6. Jeffrey Pfeffer and Gerald Salanick, *The External Control of Organizations: A Resource Dependence Perspective* (New York: Harper and Row, 1978).
7. Alfred Chandler, *The Visible Hand: The Managerial Revolution in American Business* (Cambridge: Cambridge University Press, 1977).
8. See Anthony Downs's discussion of the importance of informal communication in *Inside Bureaucracy* (Boston: Little, Brown, 1967).
9. See the discussion in Rosalyn Higgins, "The New United Nations and Former Yugoslavia," *International Affairs* 69 (1993), pp. 465-83, esp. pp. 479-80.
10. Anthony Aust, "The Procedure and Practice of the Security Council Today," in *Peacekeeping and Peacebuilding: The Development of the Role of the Security Council*, Hague Academy of International Law workshop, The Hague, 21-23 July 1992. (Dordrecht, Neth.: Martinus Nijhoff Publishers, 1993); Cameron R. Hume, *The United Nations, Iran, and Iraq* (Bloomington, Ind.: Indiana University Press, 1994).
11. Bruno Simma, ed., *The Charter of the United Nations: A Commentary* (Oxford: Oxford University Press, 1994).
12. Richard Hiscocks, *The Security Council: A Study in Adolescence* (London: Longman, 1973).
13. Isabelle Grunberg, "The 'Two Congresses': Raising Funds at Home and Abroad for the Persian Gulf War," paper presented to the European Consortium for Political Research conference at Heidelberg, September 1992; Joseph Janning "A German Europe—A European Germany? On the Debate over Germany's Foreign Policy," *International Affairs* 72 (1996), pp. 33-41.
14. See for instance the interesting if dated discussion in Richard L. Jackson, *The Non-Aligned, the United Nations, and the Superpowers* (New York: Praeger, 1983), esp. chap. 8.
15. Samar Sen, "The Rise in Importance of the Non-aligned Group" in Davidson Nicol, ed., *Paths to Peace: The United Nations Security Council and Its Presidency* (New York: Pergamon Press, 1981).
16. Jackson, *The Non-Aligned and the UN, and the Superpowers*, pp. 119-22.
17. S/PRST/1994/22, 3 May 1994. Other relevant reports, statements, and resolutions include S/PRST/1994/62, A/49/621, A/RES/49/37, and S/PRST/1996/13.
18. In fact, however, this status benefit is partly offset in the Japanese case by the popular fear that a Security Council seat would necessarily lead to an increased

international military role for the country. For survey data from Japan on this issue, see *Los Angeles Times,* 1 August 1995, p. 4.
19. On participation and legitimacy, see Giandomenico Picco, "The UN at Fifty: Reforming Institutions or Individuals?" *The World Today* 51 (1995), pp. 206-7.
20. Nomi Morris, "Buying Time: The Canadians Have Landed for a Perilous Haiti Mission," *Maclean's,* 1 April, 1996, p. 30.

8

BREAKING THE RESTRUCTURING LOGJAM

BRUCE RUSSETT, BARRY O'NEILL,
AND JAMES S. SUTTERLIN

As the United Nations Security Council became more important following the end of the Cold War, many countries asserted with new intensity their dissatisfaction with what they considered the Council's unrepresentative character and arrogant exercise of power. They directed their complaints particularly toward its five permanent members. Japan, with the status of a global economic power and second largest contributor to the United Nations, pressed for permanent membership, as did Germany. The great majority of member states called for change in the make-up of the Council and in the way it conducted its business.

As noted at the opening of Sutterlin's chapter, the General Assembly responded to the widespread demands by placing on its agenda the "Question of equitable representation on and increase in the membership of the Security Council." In December 1992 it invited member states to submit written comments "on a possible review of the membership of the Security Council." More than one hundred states provided their views.[1] The positions of some of the more influential states are listed in the appendix to this chapter. The responses vary widely; some were limited to the question of membership, while others went further to such issues as increased transparency, closer cooperation between the Security Council and the General Assembly, wider consultations with concerned parties including regional organizations, and limitation of the right of veto enjoyed by the permanent members. Underlying them all, however, were one or more of the following objectives: (1) to make the Security Council more representative of the UN membership; (2) to achieve greater international status for certain states or their representatives; (3) to augment the power of the countries of the Southern hemisphere; and (4) to lessen, through expansion of the Council, the perceived monopoly of power by the present permanent members.

In the open-ended Working Group, established by the General Assembly to consider members' comments, there has been general overt agreement that the Security Council should be enlarged and the number of permanent members increased. But as soon as the discussion becomes concrete, considering how many states should be added, or which ones, any apparent consensus evaporates. After nearly three years the Working Group has been unable to agree on these central and unavoidable issues. If the logjam is to be broken, it is time to review various proposals from the point of view of the interests they represent and try to design a package that would respond to at least the minimum interests of all. In doing so we recapitulate major points from previous chapters, and seek to integrate several perspectives.

Legitimacy, Efficiency, and Effectiveness

The Charter empowers the Security Council to act for the maintenance of international peace and security, and requires member states to comply with its decisions. This mandate is not under challenge. What is in question is whether the authority of the Council can long endure if its structure remains unchanged and, conversely, whether in an enlarged form it would retain the efficiency and effectiveness on which its authority also depends. No dominant state or coalition of powerful states is likely to be able to coerce all other sovereign states to obey its commands. It must be able to manufacture consent on the basis of its legitimacy; that is, when subordinate states recognize it as having some right, derived from principles of shared norms and representation, to issue authoritative rules.[2] Most states want an efficient Security Council, one able to reach informed, judicious, timely decisions. They also want a Council that can command the necessary financial, military, and diplomatic support from all member states to implement its decisions effectively. Whereas concern for efficiency argues for a relatively small Council, concern for an effective Council may require a larger membership. The future authority of the institution is likely to depend not only on the wisdom of its decisions, but on a reasonable distribution of power, a sharing of satisfaction, and a sense of participation across a varied range of members. Nonimplementation of its decisions (as happened regularly in the past) can undermine the credibility of the institution fully as much as can actions that are widely perceived as unwise or hostile. Ultimately, legitimacy and effectiveness depend substantially on each other.

The Cold War severely limited the operability of the Council for more than four decades, and so precluded any sustained testing of this design. The test came suddenly when, after many years of hostility, the United States and the Soviet Union found some common interest in resolving regional conflicts and when, simultaneously, they loosened the control they had exercised in third countries.

The Security Council became extremely active and severely challenged. It has authorized an unprecedented number and range of peacekeeping operations, meets in almost continuous session, passes an average of 50 resolutions a year (compared with 12 per year until 1990), and has become a powerful actor in conflict situations. Yet, at a time when conflict stems predominantly from economic and social conditions, the Council, as an essentially political body, is shadowed by uncertainty as to how the United Nations can mobilize economic resources in the pursuit of political objectives. The question implicit in the comments submitted by so many member states is whether the Council can meet the unprecedented current and future challenges while structured essentially as it was 50 years ago and following procedures that, aside from increased reliance on informal consultations, have remained remarkably unchanged.

The Security Council operates today in the context of an inherent contradiction. The relatively high degree of accord among the five permanent members has permitted the Council to take decisions with an efficiency not heretofore known. Yet the wisdom of some decisions, such as those concerning Somalia and the former Yugoslavia, has been questionable. Concerns for decision-making efficacy clash with those for legitimacy. It seems inevitable that in time the authority of the Council will decline if its composition remains unchanged. The dilemma is how to resolve that contradiction without weakening the newly achieved capacity of the UN often to act decisively, if not always wisely, on behalf of international peace and human security. Here we review and sometimes elaborate the considerations raised earlier in this volume. In doing so we raise explicitly or implicitly many of the "balances" proffered in chapter two (most obviously that between power or effectiveness and legitimacy, but also for instance, those between practicality and vision, specificity and plasticity of the Charter, and regarding the balance of interests).

Representativeness

The Security Council today is unrepresentative, in two senses:

First, from a geopolitical standpoint, of the five permanent members four are European or European-associated (the United States). Only China is considered a developing country. None is from the Southern hemisphere. Of the Council membership as a whole, 46 percent of the states are European or European-associated although this area contains only 20 percent of the world's population. Yet the UN as a whole is now numerically dominated by postcommunist and postcolonial states, many plagued by poverty and ethnic violence. Such states often lack the institutional and financial resources to deal with their problems, and understandably fear that the developed states, with great financial and military power, will try to control them. The very effectiveness of the Council has engendered fear of domination by the Five, especially the United States, at the cost of other states' sovereignty. Similarly, the dissatisfaction among developing countries with the veto power of the permanent members has increased markedly as the nonrepresentative nature of the Council has become more pronounced.

Secondly, in a quite contrary perspective, the Council is no longer representative of those countries with the greatest capacity to contribute to the maintenance of international peace and security as the founders intended. The United States, the United Kingdom, the USSR, France, and China were made permanent members of the Council in 1945 as the most powerful countries at the time and the ones expected to bear the brunt of defending peace with their armed forces. In 1945 legitimacy derived from winning the war; now legitimacy accrues more to those who can prevent or end wars. Germany and Japan, and a number of non-aligned countries, have a history of important contributions to conflict prevention and peacebuilding. Perhaps sympathetic attention to Security Council expansion is a touchstone of the great powers' seriousness about containing potential epidemics of violence.

If economic strength is given its full weight, two other states—Germany and Japan—together are now able to offer a contribution to the maintenance of international security comparable to that of the U.S., and far greater than any of the others. Indeed, under the assessment formula that requires permanent members to pay a "premium" above the share that their wealth would impose, new permanent members would acquire responsibility for an increased share of the peacekeeping budget, bringing a consequent reduction in the American share. Japan, as the second largest economic power and second largest contributor to the U.N., is making a strong case for permanent membership on the ground of "taxation with representation." Germany has staked a similar claim. Concerns about their political and constitutional ability (especially Japan's) to carry the full responsibilities of peacekeeping and enforcement somewhat hinder their efforts. Moreover, the campaigns of these Northern industrial countries for permanent membership only strengthen the demands of Southern developing countries for representation based on the principle of equitable geographical distribution or, in some cases, population. Nevertheless, if Germany and Japan are denied this status, their willingness to make the large financial contributions needed, and ultimately greater military ones as well, will likely be undermined. If so, the effectiveness of the Council will suffer.

Power

Power—the ability to determine outcomes—is the most obvious stake in the contest over the Council's composition. In international relations, a state's power is derived in various degrees from its economic strength, its military capabilities, its diplomatic skill and command of information, and its ideological legitimacy. The United States, for the achievement of most of its goals, would be the most powerful state in the international system whether or not there were a United Nations. Its status as a permanent member of the Security Council, and so its capacity to influence decisions of that body, adds to this ability. Understandably, other states would like whatever power that membership on the Council might bring them. The amount of power potentially accruing to them depends both on their basic strength outside the UN, and on the composition and voting rules of the Security Council itself.[3]

The power of the United States in the Security Council, for example, stems in large part from its inherent capabilities as a superpower. It can often persuade other members of the Council to vote with it from common principles of ideology and world order, or through rewards of side payments, or by implicit or explicit threats of punishment. States without a seat on the Council may have some ways of influencing actual members, but they lack this most obvious source of power. Hence we see demands for increasing the total number of members of the Council, variously to a size of from 20 to 30 states. Especially given the reservation of five seats to the permanent members, the chance for most states to secure a Security Council seat, even of the two-year variety, within the lifetime of their diplomats is slim indeed. An expanded Council might fatten that chance slightly.

Once a state is on the Council, its formal power over decisions depends on the voting rules, as shown in the chapter by O'Neill. One must consider both the ability to accomplish something (to get a resolution adopted) and the ability to prevent it (to see to it that a resolution is not adopted). In a body operating on the principle of a simple majority, every member has, in theory, equal power both to accomplish and power to prevent. If, however, some states have a veto, their affirmative vote, or at the least an abstention, is always essential to adoption of a resolution. Thus they gain a substantial blocking capability denied to ordinary members.

The mere possibility of casting a veto gives a state benefits whether or not it actually does block a resolution's passage. The threat to veto a resolution is usually an effective means of demanding that the resolution be modified, or of obtaining side payments. As a defensive mechanism, however, the value of the veto depends on the number of allies a country has in the Council. The United States did not find it necessary to use the veto before 1970 since, until then, it could rally enough support from others to prevent a resolution that it opposed from coming to a vote. During this same period, the USSR had to use the veto 105 times, because it was isolated and only through the veto could it prevent the adoption of resolutions that were contrary to its interests. Since 1970, however, the United States has made use of the veto 70 times and the USSR/Russian Federation only 19 times, reflecting very clearly the relationship between the value of the veto and the degree of isolation of a permanent member on substantive issues.[4]

A simple counting of the use of the veto is a deceptive indicator of the power gained by a state through access to the veto. Since 1989 only three vetoes have been cast. One was in May 1995 by the United States on a resolution criticizing Israel. The other two were by Russia. But the threat of a veto often sufficed to influence the Council majority as reflected in the draft resolution itself. Indeed, Russia reportedly exercised the veto in one of these two recent instances (a minor budgetary matter) mainly to demonstrate that it was still willing to use its privilege and thus reinforce the credibility of its threat. Because China is so "distant" from the ideological center of gravity of other permanent members, the possibility of a veto by China is the most credible, even though it has seldom cast one. China has used implicit or explicit threats of a veto to extract side payments on issues such as trade and human rights. Its frequent abstentions make the point, without actually blocking a resolution. As shown earlier, most of the abstentions concerned resolutions invoking enforcement action under Chapter VII, and actions that the Chinese government deemed intervention in the internal affairs of sovereign states. In the current situation China stands to benefit most from using the veto threat as a lever to gain its policy ends.

Discussion of the veto alone can obscure the second way in which the Security Council diverges from the majority rule principle. The number of affirmative votes required to pass a resolution is more than a simple majority. Under the current Charter provision, 9 of the 15 members must approve a resolution. If only a simple majority were required, the permanent 5 (assuming none abstained) would need just 3 votes from the remaining 10 members to pass a resolution. To reach the total of 9, they must persuade 4 others to agree. Thus the higher action threshold slightly increases the power of nonpermanent members over what they would have under a simple majority rule. But only slightly. When the permanent members do stick together, it is seldom hard to persuade enough nonpermanent ones to go along. The power of a nonpermanent member in this circumstance would be manifested less in actually casting a negative vote than in some ability, in competition with other potential "sellers," to extract some side payments in return for its affirmative vote. Small states may seek membership so as to acquire such leverage.

Voting rules can produce subtle and complex effects. At least by the method of analysis employed in O'Neill's chapter, in the current Security Council configuration each permanent member with a veto in the Security Council possesses immensely greater voting power than does each of the nonpermanent members. In these strict voting power terms, permanent membership with a veto is what really counts. A restriction of the scope of issues on which a veto can be cast, or a big rise in the voting threshold, would be required to materially diminish the veto's importance.

Alliances and voting blocs, however, require an important qualification to this simple picture. The United States, for example, has had many reliable allies in the Security Council—the United Kingdom, France, to some degree Russia among the permanent members, and recently the Czech Republic, Germany, Italy, and usually Argentina among nonpermanent members. Thus this bloc, when united, needed to find only one more vote among the remaining seven. Those seven include China and the members of the Non-Aligned Movement who vote with it in the General Assembly (Botswana, Honduras, Indonesia, Nigeria, Oman, and Rwanda). When China votes affirmatively, *none* of the others are needed; if China chose to abstain, then any one of the smaller states would suffice. If the non-aligned states could stick together as a solid bloc they could sometimes exercise a "sixth veto" and as a group have the same power as one of the permanent members. But the temptations or pressures on one or more of them to break any such solidarity are immense.[5] If one state is tempted to resist, it knows that another is likely to succumb. Neither as a group nor as individuals do they have much power.

The voting bloc effect thus means that the impact of adding new permanent members with veto rights depends heavily on who is added. Germany and Japan vote regularly with other rich industrial states in the General Assembly and in the Security Council when they happen to hold nonpermanent seats. *So long as their alignment in international politics holds relatively constant* (and assuming they do not themselves ever become potential targets of collective restraint), their acquisition of permanent (and veto-wielding) membership would not fundamentally alter the balance of political forces on the Council. Anything they might wish to veto probably would be opposed by Britain, France, and/or the United States anyway. Giving such membership to members of the Non-Aligned Movement (for example, India, Nigeria, or to a lesser degree Brazil), however, would greatly complicate efforts to pass resolutions. With the Cold War East-West division now in the past, the basic structure of alignment in the UN derives from the remaining North-South fissure. On North-South issues a new non-aligned permanent member would be likely to have substantive views quite different from those of the developed Northern countries and more like those of China. The Northern states would have to deal not only with a Chinese veto threat, but with the possibility of a veto by one or more of these other new members as well. It is hardly surprising that the present United States position on Security Council enlargement is that the total not exceed 20, of which Germany and Japan would be the only new permanent members (probably with veto).

The effect of expanding the number of nonpermanent members, or of the non-aligned states in particular, would depend also on what adjustments were made to the action threshold. The permanent members might need more votes from the nonpermanent members, but have a wider pool of nonpermanent members from whom to obtain support. A widely unappreciated result of the 1965 expansion of the Council illustrates the complications. The total membership of the Council rose from 11 to 15, with 4 new nonpermanent members. The required majority went up only from 7 to 9, meaning that a lower percentage of affirmative votes was needed after expansion (60 percent) than before (63.6 percent). On balance it was easier for the permanent members to find the remaining votes they needed. Nevertheless, the increase in nonpermanent members also made it easier for the non-aligned to find a nine-vote majority in favor of a resolution opposed by the U.S., and thus to force the United States to use the veto. This technique was followed occasionally on issues pertaining to the Middle East. Similarly, while the United States could usually obtain modification of a resolution by threatening to veto, it was often forced to accept wording it disliked so as to *avoid* using the veto with the adverse political fallout that would entail.

The consequences of any expansion of the Security Council therefore are tied not only to the total numbers, the number of states with veto rights, and precisely which states are added. It also matters what action threshold is required, and what purposes member states pursue.

Having power on the Security Council is not the same as being satisfied with its decisions. A state not a member of the Council—and thus without formal power on it—may nevertheless be satisfied if it has allies on the Council who generally are able to pass resolutions that it favors or who can block resolutions it dislikes. To the extent that the Security Council majority reflects a majority in the General Assembly as well, then most UN members will be satisfied with resolutions that are passed, and dissatisfied when they are blocked by a minority or a veto.

Voting power on the Council can even be a liability if, for example, a state is seen as therefore having special responsibilities for supporting a peacekeeping action. If a state lacks domestic consensus on what course of action it should pursue in a particular instance, its government may find membership on the Council to be a political liability. Voting power can also make a small state the focus of influence attempts. Yemen may well have regretted being a member of the Council during the Gulf War, as it was pressured by both sides for its support and suffered retribution from the United States and some Arab states afterwards. Therefore power is not always the ultimate goal.

This fact, plus the minuscule power that joining confers on the nonpermanent members, suggests that other motives lie behind many countries' desire for Council enlargement. Their motives may include participation, prestige, respect, legitimacy, equality: often largely symbolic goals. But symbolism is much of what politics is about. The importance of these other motives suggests that it may be possible to devise creative ways of addressing them while still satisfying current members' concerns about protecting the veto and preserving the Council's efficiency and effectiveness.

The concern for maintaining an efficient Security Council remains central. A Council hobbled by new veto-wielding or veto-threatening states might not act quickly or decisively in a crisis, or perhaps could not act at all. Much the same result could be produced if there were a substantial enlargement even of just the nonpermanent membership, or a serious increase in the majority threshold. Either of these would greatly complicate the task of assembling sufficient votes to pass a resolution. A major change in the veto, such as with a weighted voting scheme as suggested in chapter six, would require extremely complex negotiations on the formula, and seems too much to attempt. Moreover, if set high enough to protect the voting power of the current permanent members it would in effect mean extending the veto to most or all of the new permanent members.

In the long run, of course, the rise of new issues may break apart current alignments, or political changes may cause states to find new friends and face new enemies. The ability to cast a veto thus functions as an insurance policy even for states which do not make much use of it at the moment. Even the United States has to be concerned with the possibility that it might badly need the veto in some future international climate. By the same token, it might someday regret adding new veto-wielding states to the Council even though those states are now reliable friends. A veto is forever.

Why Change Is Difficult

The primary obstacle to change in the size and composition of the Security Council is constitutional, embedded in Article 108: "Amendments to the present Charter shall come into force for all members of the United Nations when they have been adopted by a vote of two-thirds of the members of the General Assembly and ratified in accordance with their respective constitutional processes by two-thirds of the members of the United Nations, including all the permanent members of the Council."

Charter amendment is essential to any change in the composition of the Security Council. No change can be achieved without the formal consent of all the veto powers. But neither can it be achieved without the consent of two-thirds of all UN members. In effect, a change needs the support of virtually all the North and about half of the non-aligned states. This will be difficult to achieve, given the wide disparity of states' and groups preferences as indicated in the appendix to this chapter.

Of the permanent 5, the United States, as noted, has expressed strong support for adding Germany and Japan as permanent members, and up to three more nonpermanent members. It has also called for setting the required majority at 12, 60 percent of an expanded Council of 20. Consequently, instead of 5 permanent members needing to find 4 out of 10 nonpermanent votes as at present, in the new Council the 7 permanent members would need 5 nonpermanent votes out of 13. Even if 3 of the permanent members abstained, only 8 nonpermanent votes would be required. The job of finding support would be easier, and the voting power of nonpermanent members, as defined above, would be even less than its current minuscule value.

The United States position has not been pushed very hard by Washington. It is likely a nonstarter. First of all, granting permanent membership only to Japan and Germany, and thereby increasing the already disproportionate representation of the industrialized North, is unacceptable to the non-aligned majority in the UN. If Germany and Japan are given permanent membership, the addition of a limited number of nonpermanent seats will in no way satisfy the South. Nor is the American position necessarily intended to get very far. Despite the Clinton and previously the Bush administrations' wish to satisfy German and Japanese aspirations, expansion of the Security Council can hardly be a high priority in Washington at the moment. The present administration has enough on its hands fending off Congressional attacks on the UN as a whole and trying to maintain the immediate efficacy of the Council.

Britain and France have also indicated support for the addition of Germany and Japan as permanent members. One idea for doing this without enlarging the total number of permanent members has been to substitute for French and U.K. membership a European Union permanent seat to be jointly controlled or occupied sequentially by Britain, France, and Germany (and possibly Italy, which is not eager to see Germany elevated to permanent membership). Such a change would permit permanent membership for Japan without adding to the number of permanent members or altering the proportionate representation of the North. Not surprisingly, the British and French governments categorically reject the proposal.

Russia has expressed willingness to see the Council enlarged without setting a specific number. It supports permanent membership for Germany and Japan, but only if India is also given this status. China has not gone much beyond a general statement of support for an enlarged Council. Presumably it is not keen to see India, a long-term regional rival, achieve permanent membership. Moreover, with India's elevation China would lose its presently unique role as the only representative able to defend the South with a veto—valuable for influence with the non-aligned as well as for extracting side payments from other permanent members.

The positions taken by Japan and Germany serve to illustrate the extreme difficulty of finding a formula for Council enlargement even when, as is now the case, there is unanimous stated agreement that the Council should be enlarged. The two countries both propose that the number of permanent members be increased to 10 to include themselves and 3 members selected on a regional basis. The total size of the Council would be increased to 23, thus also providing room for additional non-aligned rotating members. However, the proposal is dependent on the ability of the three regions—Africa, Asia, and Latin America—to agree on a mechanism by which the General Assembly would ultimately allocate the permanent seats reserved for them. Would the regional representative itself be permanent, or merely the status of the region, with the actual representative changing? As to the former, the discussions in the General Assembly Working Group have shown there is little possibility that the three regional groups can reach agreement on which three countries among them should be given permanent membership. Would Pakistan accept Indian elevation to permanent status? Would Argentina and Mexico accept that of Brazil? Would Nigeria—powerful, politically unstable, and currently undemocratic—attract the support of many of its neighbors? If the regional groups cannot agree, the Germans hold that Germany and Japan should alone be added as permanent members.

Nor are any of the current permanent members prepared to consider surrendering their veto power, though that would make the addition of new Northern permanent members less offensive to the South. The idea of granting permanent membership to additional countries without the right of veto has attracted interest. For the United States (which has indicated openness to the idea) and for others, this formula could make the elevation of several Southern countries to permanent membership less objectionable and could possibly give some satisfaction to friendly powers without raising fears of decreased effectiveness by extending the veto. It could seemingly satisfy in part the desire of Germany and Japan to be recognized as major and legitimate actors on the international scene. But it would not provide a basis of "equal rights," nor, considering the difference in voting power between those who have a veto and those who don't, should anyone expect them, or any of the non-aligned aspirants, to favor such a compromise. Both Japan and Germany have rejected it, for the present at least. The same is true of proposals for new permanent members to have "half a veto"; i.e, two of them would have to vote together to constitute an actual veto. Rather than accept any such partial loaves now, they may prefer to take their chances on a full loaf a decade or two in the future. Proposals for weighted voting, as put forth in chapter six, seem beyond the bounds of negotiating practicality.

On top of all this is the fear of many Southern states that any great expansion of permanent membership will simply make it less likely that they ever will achieve a term as nonpermanent members. In February 1995 the Non-Aligned Movement consequently called for enlarging the Security Council to at least 26, a number above that contemplated by any of the Northern members concerned with maintaining the effectiveness of the Council.

Breaking the Logjam

It is hard to see how any of the current proposals can be adopted. Possibly there is enough support to bring to a vote a proposal for adding Germany and Japan as permanent members, alone or with others. The current permanent members might well accept it, but the prospects of putting together a two-thirds majority of General Assembly members behind it are very dim. In such a complex choice situation as this one, the chances for success depend very much on the order in which particular proposals are considered. A proposal that might under some circumstances gain acquiescence can easily fail if it is presented too soon or too late in the process. Perhaps some omniscient Game Overall Director could devise just the right sequencing to eliminate options and produce some solution that enough states would accept. Even She, however, might find the puzzle insoluble. For the problem at hand, for virtually every proposal one state or another, or a group of states, appears to have an ability, and an interest, to obstruct any particular change. For some, the status quo is quite satisfactory, and better than any change other than one that specifically gives them more power. Yet any long extension of the status quo carries serious dangers, and for many states is not acceptable.

If expansion of the permanent membership of the Security Council is out of the question—with or without veto power to the new members—other elements of a possible package must come into play. And while the package will hardly delight anyone, it must have something to please, in some degree, all the numerous players who have the ability to block its adoption. The power to affect passage of a resolution is a zero-sum game. For every gain to one or more states, others must lose, and will resist that loss. But voting power is not everything. States not given much formal power may nevertheless be satisfied by reforms that give them greater respect, a sense of larger participation in decision making, a perception that the Council is more representative, and an expectation that it will be able to take effective decisions of which they largely approve.

We are not optimistic about the prospects for major change in the Council's composition in the foreseeable future. Nevertheless we suggest the following elements of a package that might at some point look feasible. Substantial agreement that most or all the following dimensions must be addressed as a comprehensive package has emerged in the General Assembly Working Group.

1. Eliminate the Charter provision in Article 23(2) that prohibits the immediate reelection of a nonpermanent member whose term has expired. This would have attraction for several big regional powers as promising more or less permanent presence on the Council. In particular, it would partially address the wishes of Germany and Japan. It is substantially less than they want, but—with some other concessions identified below—might suffice.[6]
2. Expand the nonpermanent membership (including any of the above) to 16, for a total Council body of 21. Given the vastly enlarged membership of the UN, some such expansion of the Council is essential to meet the wish of smaller states for some greater opportunity to serve as members, particularly if two or more states can be expected to gain near-perpetual status. There is no clearly identifiable threshold at which the body would become unwieldy, but—other things being equal—less is better than more. Although a total of 21 begins to push the limits of what some see as a Council that can be efficient in the conditions of international military and political crisis, it would still be a reasonably manageable body.
3. Raise the action threshold, or number of affirmative votes needed to pass a resolution, perhaps to 13 or even 14 of the 21. The lower number (61.9 percent of the total) would be above the current 60 percent but a bit below the percentage before the 1965 Council expansion; the higher (66.7 percent) would be substantially higher. Even the lower number would compel the 5 permanent members to acquire 8 out of the 16 nonpermanents for any winning coalition—a harder job than the current task of gaining 4 out of 10. While no one should be deluded into thinking that any such increment to the power of nonpermanent members would be more than marginal, it could offer some modest improvement for the non-aligned. This possibility has received relatively little attention so far, and could constitute an element to help break the impasse.
4. Restrict the scope of the veto, in some manner. The veto was originally intended to protect the vital interests of those great powers whose assent to UN actions for peace and security was essential to the viability of the organization. In practice the veto right has been abused, employed over a much wider range of

substantive concerns, including the admission of new members and even election of the Secretary-General. One way to attack the veto problem is to consider limiting its applicability only to enforcement measures proposed under Chapter VII, or to other decisions entailing the use of military force. But the existing permanent members will vigorously resist any restriction on the veto. The United States clearly makes use of the veto threat for the Secretary-General's election.[7] Yet if some kind of restriction could be agreed upon it might be a small and acceptable price to get the rest of the package, and could probably be achieved through a joint resolution by the permanent members, without formal Charter amendment.

5. Delete Article 107, referring to "any state which during the Second World War has been an enemy of any signatory to the present Charter" and modify Article 53 to remove a similar reference. These provisions are uniformly viewed as anachronistic and have been officially renounced by the United States and the USSR as they refer to Germany, Japan, and Italy. However, they remain an affront to those countries and to smaller states that were once their allies. This loose end should be snipped off.[8]

6. Accompany these changes by a resolution of the Security Council expressing the decision:

   a) to take further measures to increase the transparency of the Council's operation;
   b) to collaborate more closely with the General Assembly on security matters, including disarmament;
   c) to engage in wide consultations with concerned parties, including regional organizations;
   d) to reexamine the structure and composition of the Security Council by periodic review at specified times, beginning perhaps 15 years hence.

How do these add up for each of the major groups?

- Germany and Japan do not get permanent membership or a veto. But with likely successive reelection they achieve semipermanent status, and with the scope of the veto somewhat reduced, their deprivation is less. Repeal of the enemy clauses and

reexamination of the Council's composition in 15 years offer some small benefits, at no cost to others.
- All the current permanent members sacrifice a little scope of their formal veto power, but some of them might even gain from restricting others' ability to cast vetoes. Otherwise none of them loses much of any substance.
- The South derives modest gains from restricting the veto, increasing consultation and transparency, and raising the required action threshold.
- Most of these gains are largely symbolic, with no one a serious loser. The balance of power is not tipped markedly in anyone's favor. The efficiency of the Council is essentially preserved, which would not be likely if the veto power were extended to new members or if the total membership of the Council were enlarged above 21.

Will such a comprehensive, a-little-for-everyone agreement be easy to get? Hardly. Several of the elements—expanding the nonpermanent membership and enacting a new voting percentage formula, permitting immediate reelection, and removing the enemy states clauses—can be achieved only by Charter amendment. But the first two have been done once before, in 1965, and these amendments do not directly confront the basic national interests that most legislatures will be concerned to protect in the ratification process. The alternatives to change look worse. Despite the Organization's ability to evolve and adapt informally to changing power realities, staying indefinitely with the Charter status quo cannot be satisfactory. No institution can afford to continue without any structural adjustments if the circumstances in which it operates undergo fundamental change. Every constitution must strike some balance between stability and adaptability. Without change its acceptance, and ultimately its effectiveness, will be eroded.

APPENDIX

Major States' Public Positions on Expanding the Security Council (as of August 1996)

COUNTRY	PROPOSAL FOR EXPANSION
Brazil	Increase permanent members by 5 or 6 and nonpermanent members by 4 or 5; total of 25.
China	Increase membership into the low 20s; more representation of developing countries and small and medium ones.
Egypt	Endorses NAM position; equitable geographical representation; more representation of NAM countries. Add clause for periodic review of Council composition.
France	Increase permanent members by up to 5 with veto; total membership of 20 or 21. New permanent members to include Germany, Japan, and possibly developing countries.
Germany	Increase by 5 permanent members, probably with veto, and 4 or 5 nonpermanent members from Africa, Asia, Latin America, and Eastern Europe.
India	Increase membership by at least 11, including at least 5 new permanent members with veto.
Italy	Create 10 nonpermanent seats, each of which would rotate among 3 countries. Each would pay a surcharge for peacekeeping. Retain ban on immediate reelection of existing members. Limit scope of veto, or require 2 negative votes to constitute a veto.

Breaking the Restructuring Logjam

Japan	Increase permanent members by up to 5, with veto.
Mexico	Increase nonpermanent members by 5; one each for Africa, Asia, and Latin America; one to alternate between Western Europe and Other State group and Eastern Europe; one to alternate between Germany and Japan. Require 2 negative votes to constitute a veto.
Nigeria	Increase of 5 permanent members with veto, 2 each for Africa and Asia, and one for Latin America. Accommodate Germany through an adjustment involving the European Union. Phase out the veto.
Russia	Increase membership into the low 20s, no specification how the new seats would be allocated.
South Africa	Probably increase membership by 11, including 6 new permanent members, 2 each for Africa, Asia, and Latin America.
United Kingdom	Germany and Japan to have permanent membership with veto. Supports new seats for developing countries without yet specifying whether permanent members or not.
United States	Germany and Japan to have permanent membership, plus 3 new nonpermanent members; perhaps remove the ban on reelection.
Non-Aligned Movement	Increase membership by at least 11; with at least 4 new seats each for Africa and Asia, and 3 for Latin America. Perhaps only new nonpermanent members. If some permanent, include developing as well as developed countries.
Nordic Countries (5)	Increase permanent members by 5 and nonpermanent members by 3; retain ban on immediate reelection.

NOTE: Public positions are not necessarily what each state in fact hopes or wishes to achieve.

We are grateful to Sam Daws of Oxford University for supplying this information.

NOTES

1. A full compilation of comments of member states is contained in the report of the Secretary-General to the 48th session of the General Assembly, A/48/264.
2. See Lea Brilmayer, *American Hegemony: Political Morality in a One-Superpower World* (New Haven, Conn.: Yale University Press, 1994).
3. David Caron, "The Legitimacy of the Collective Authority of the Security Council," *American Journal of International Law* 87 (1993), pp. 552-88.
4. No official count is kept by the United Nations of the use by a country of the veto. Unofficial counts and national counts vary considerably. This results in part from varying practices in counting vetoes when more than one permanent member casts a negative vote on a draft resolution. The U.S. and the U.K. frequently have both voted negatively on a resolution, sometimes also with France. As far as UN records are concerned, a resolution fails because of the negative vote of a permanent member regardless of how many permanent members vote no.
5. No instance of an actual "sixth veto" is evident. The threat of one can, however, sometimes force substantial revision, as occurred in Resolution 748 on sanctions against Libya.
6. The major difficulty here is that, with the existing provision of two-year terms for nonpermanent members, they would effectively be in a continuous and never-ending campaign for reelection. An alternative might be to make only some of the new nonpermanent seats eligible for immediate reelection, for terms of four or six years. To extend the term for all nonpermanent seats while also removing the ban on reelection for all would so limit the possibilities of many small states ever to get a seat as likely to be unacceptable to them.
7. The Independent Working Group on the Future of the United Nations, *The United Nations in Its Second Half-Century* (New York: Ford Foundation, 1995) suggested limiting the veto applicability to Chapter VII questions. In not recommending the addition of any new permanent members we depart from the Working Group, though they too recognize the barriers to adding new veto members by saying (p. 16), "A change in the use of the veto... would be in order even if no alternation is made in the Council's membership." On the current role of the veto in elections of the Secretary-General there is some ambiguity. Article 97 of the Charter provides that he "shall be appointed by the General Assembly upon the recommendation of the Security Council," and in all cases of initial election of a Secretary-General the veto has been operative, forcing a compromise among the permanent members for their recommendation to the Assembly. But in 1950, faced with a Soviet veto of a new full term for Trygve Lie, and no Security Council recommendation, the Assembly extended Lie's term of office for three years. The U.S. 1996 veto of Boutros-Ghali stood.
8. The Special Committee on the Charter of the United Nations and the Strengthening of the Organization, at the 1995 session, recommended that the General Assembly should express its intention to initiate, at the earliest appropriate future session, the procedure to amend the Charter with a view to deleting the "enemy states" clauses. A/50/33.

CONTRIBUTORS

Ian Hurd, a citizen of Canada, holds a B.A. from Carleton University and is now a Ph.D. candidate at Yale studying the United Nations and other international institutions.

Soo Yeon Kim, a citizen of the Republic of Korea, holds a B.A. from Yonsei University and an M.A. from the University of Houston. Now a Ph.D. candidate in political science at Yale, her dissertation is on *Bilateral Conflict and Trade, 1948–1993*.

Barry O'Neill, a citizen of Canada, is Associate Professor of Management and Political Science at Yale. His book, *Honor, Signals, and War*, will be published in 1997 by the University of Michigan Press. He is a specialist on bargaining and negotiation, and a frequent contributor to journals and books concerned with game theory and international relations.

Bruce Russett is Dean Acheson Professor of Political Science and Director of United Nations Studies at Yale, and Editor of the *Journal of Conflict Resolution*. He served with Paul Kennedy as co-director of the Secretariat for the Independent Working Group's report, *The United Nations in Its Second Half-Century,* presented to Boutros Boutros-Ghali in June 1995. A past president of the International Studies Association and the Peace Science Society (International), he is author or editor of 20 other books and has published many articles.

James S. Sutterlin is Distinguished Fellow of United Nations Studies at Yale. He was formerly Executive Director of the Executive Office of the Secretary General, and recently served as Chair of the Academic Council on the United Nations System. His recent publications include *The United Nations and the Maintenance of International Peace and Security,* and he has been assisting Javier Pérez de Cuéllar in the preparation of his memoirs. He directs an oral history project on the United Nations.

Masayuki Tadokoro is Professor of International Relations at Himeji-Dokkyo University. He holds LL.B. and LL.M. degrees from the University of Kyoto, and also studied at the London School of Economics and Political Science. He has been a visiting scholar at several universities in England and the United States as well as in Japan. His most recent books include *The United Nations Budget* (in Japanese) and *People: From Impoverishment to Empowerment* (in English).

Nigel Thalakada, a native of Sri Lanka, holds a B.A. from the University of Virginia and an M.Phil. from Cambridge University. He is currently a Ph.D. candidate in political science at Yale.

INDEX

Afghanistan, 6
Alesina, Alberto, 28nn.12, 13
Alker, Hayward R., Jr., 30, 56nn.1, 2, 3, 7, 58n.15
Angola, 102
Aristide, Jean-Bertrand, 6, 93
Aust, Anthony, 151n.10
Awanohara, Susumu, 118n.34

Bailey, Sidney D., 151n.3
Baker, James, 104
Banzhaf, John, 80n.5
Barnett, Michael, 27n.6
Belgium, 4
Bertram, Eva, 28n.18
Bosnia-Herzegovina, 24, 99-100, 102, 121; China's position on, 85, 89-92, 94, 95-96, 97, 100, 101
Boutros-Ghali, Boutros, 24, 28n.16, 133n.1
Brams, Steven, 81nn.6, 8
Brazil, 160, 165
Brilmayer, Lea, 172n.2
Bull, Hedley, 27n.6
Burkhart, Ross, 28n.13
Bush, George, 104

Cambodia: China's position on, 97
Canada, 4
Caron, David, 172n.3
Carr, Edward Hallett, 20, 28n.9
Carreras, Francese, 81n.6
Castillo, Graciana del, 28n.18
Chad, 103
Chandler, Alfred, 151n.7

Childers, Erskine, 27n.2
China, ix; abstentions on Chapter VII resolutions, 88-95; abstentions on non-Chapter VII resolutions, 95-98; affirmative votes on Chapter VII resolutions, 98-103; economic development goals, 103; foreign policy objectives, 84-88, 106; and United States, 87-88, 104-5; veto power as used by, ix, 75-76, 159, 164; voting patterns in Security Council, ix-x, 83-84, 103-7
Chinese Communist Party (CCP), 85
Churchill, Winston, 4
civil rights, 22-23
Commission on Global Governance, 27nn.2, 4
Conference on Security and Co-operation in Europe, 96
Croatia, 100
Crossette, Barbara, 117n.23
Cuba, 105

Dahl, Robert, 60, 80n.2
Damrosch, Lori Fisler, 27n.1
Daniel, Donald C. F., 27n.1
David, Morton, 81n.8
Deagan, J., 80n.5
Deng Ziaoping: foreign policy of, 84-86
disarmament: as issue in voting alignments, 37-38, 47
Dixon, William, 80n.5

d'Orville, Hans, 28n.8
Downs, Anthony, 151n.8
Elkins, D. J., 27n.6
Emmons, Julianne, 57n.12

Fishburn, P., 81n.10
France, 4
Fulci, Francesco Paolo, 65

Gehrlein, W., 81n.10
General Assembly. *See* United Nations General Assembly
Germany: proposed as permanent member of Security Council, ix, 126, 131, 150, 153, 163-64; relations with Security Council, 144, 147
Grunberg, Isabelle, 151n.13
Gubser, Michael, 57n.13
Gulf War, 86

Haiti, 6, 86; China's position on, 93, 96, 100, 102, 149
Hayes, Brad C., 27n.1
Heckman, James, 56n.6
Helliwell, John F., 28n.13
Higgins, Rosalyn, 151n.9
Hilderbrand, Robert C., 28n.10
Hiscocks, Richard, 151n.12
Holloway, Steven, 31, 56n.6
human rights, 21-22, 38-39
Hurd, Ian, x
Hutus. *See* Rwanda
Hwei-Ling Huo, 117n.9

Independent Working Group on the Future of the United Nations, Report of, 11n.4, 15-26, 27nn.2, 4, 172n.7
India: proposed as permanent member of Security Council, 160, 164, 165
International Atomic Energy Agency, 97

International Court of Justice, 20
International Monetary Fund, 18, 125, 133n.2
Iran, 38
Iraq, 38; China's position on, 87, 88-89, 95, 97, 101, 103, 105
Islamic countries, 38-39
Italy, ix, 164

Jackson, Richard L., 151nn.14, 16
Janning, Joseph, 151n.13
Japan, 61-62; proposed as permanent member of Security Council, ix, 126, 129-31, 150, 153, 163-64; relations with Security Council, 144, 147
Joffe, George, 118n.35

Kant, Immanuel, 13, 27n.5
Kennedy, Paul, xi, 27n.5, 86, 117n.6
Khmer Rouge, 97
Kim, Samuel, 86, 105, 117nn.2, 3, 4
Kim, Soo Yeon, viii, 63, 72-74
Kirgis, Frederic L., Jr., 150n.1
Korea. *See* North Korea; South Korea
Kuroda, Tatsuaki, 80n.5
Kuwait: China's position on, 87, 88-89, 103

Lake, M., 81n.8
League of Nations: weaknesses of, 2
Levin, Richard, xi

Lewis-Beck, Michael, 28n.13
Li Yuan-zu, 96
Liberia, 4, 102
Libya, 92, 103, 104
Limongi, Fernando, 28n.13

MacRae, Duncan, 82n.12
Magana, Antonio, 81n.6
Maoz, Zeev, 27n.3
Marín-Bosch, Miguel, 57n.10
Mendez, Ruben, 28n.8

Missile Technology Control Regime, 106
Mobutu Sese Seko, 23
Morris, Nomi, 152n.20

Najman, Dragoljub, 28n.8
Nevison, Christopher, 81n.9
Newcombe, Alan G., 56n.5
Newcombe, Hanna, 56n.5
Nigeria, 160, 165
Non-Aligned Movement (NAM), 31, 65; and Security Council, 144-45, 147, 160, 165
North Atlantic Treaty Organization (NATO), 11n.1
North Korea: relations with China, 97
Nuclear Non-Proliferation Treaty, 97, 106

Olson, Mancur, 28n.14
Oneal, Frances, 27n.3
Oneal, John, 27n.3
O'Neill, Barry, ix, x-xi, 57n.9, 149, 159
Organization for Economic Cooperation and Development (OECD), 31
Organization for Security and Cooperation in Europe (OSCE), 11n.1
Owen, G., 81n.11

Packel, E., 80n.5
Park, Chi Young, 133n.3
Patil, Anjali V., 117n.1
Penketh, Anne, 118n.37
People's Republic of China. *See* China
Perotti, Roberto, 28nn.12, 13
Perrow, Charles, 151n.5
Peterson, M. J., 57n.11
Pfeffer, Jeffrey, 151n.6
Picco, Giandomenico, 152n.19
political rights, 22-23; as issue in voting alignments, 38-39, 51-52
Poole, Keith, 82n.12

Powers, Richard, 56n.5
Przeworski, Adam, 28n.13
Putnam, Robert, 28n.13

Qian Qichen, 88, 101, 104

Rapid Reaction Force, 24-25
Ratner, Steven, 27n.7
Reisman, W. Michael, 28n.11
rights. *See* civil rights; human rights; political rights
Robinson, Thomas W., 117n.7
Romania, 86
Roosevelt, Franklin, 3
Rosenthal, Howard, 82n.12
Ross, Michael, 56n.5
Rummel, R. J., 57n.8
Russett, Bruce, viii, x-xi, 27n.3, 30, 31, 56nn.3, 4, 7, 58n.15, 63, 72-74,
Russia. *See* Union of Soviet Socialist Republics
Rwanda, 24, 102; China's position on, 93-94, 97

Salanick, Gerald, 151n.6
Samar, Sen, 151n.15
Schwodiauer, Gerhard, 81n.6
Scott, W. Richard, 151n.4
Security Council. *See* United Nations Security Council
self-determination: as issue in voting alignments, 33-38, 39-43, 51
Sen, Amartya, 28n.15
Shapley, Lloyd, 60, 80nn.1, 6, 81nn.7, 11
Shapley-Shubik index, 60-61, 62, 80n.4
Shichor, Yitzhak, 118n.36
Shubik, Martin, 60, 80nn.1, 6
Simma, Bruno, 151n.11
Siverson, Randolph, 57n.12
Smith, Gaddis, xii
Snyder, James, 56n.6

Somalia, 24, 86, 99, 102, 121
Soto, Alvaro de, 28n.18
South Africa, 102
South Korea, 133n.3
Soviet Union. *See* Union of Soviet Socialist Republics
Starr, Harvey, 57n.13
states: role of international organization in, 16-17; sovereignty of, 15-17, 106; under stress, 16-17
Stettinius, Edward R., Jr., 3, 11n.2
Straffin, Philip, 60, 80n.3, 81n.8
Sudan, 38
Sutterlin, James, vii-viii, x-xi, 153

Tadokoro, Masayuki, x, 150
Taiwan, 96
Thalakada, Nigel, ix-x, 149
Tomlinson, Rodney, 56n.6
Truman, Harry, 3
Tutsis. *See* Rwanda

UNEF I, 6
Union of Soviet Socialist Republics (USSR), 4
United Nations: balancing interests within, viii, 26; coordination of agencies of, 25-26; financing of, 17-18, 124; military force as used by, 3-4, 5, 24-25; power versus legitimacy in, 18-21; proposals for reform of, vii, viii, 13-26, 79-80, 131-32; restructuring of, 120; role of in states under stress, 16-17; roles played by, 119, 131-32; vision of, 13-14. *See also* United Nations Security Council
United Nations Charter: amendments to, 25, 135, 163; Article 39, 28n.17; Article 44, 5, 11n.3, 146; Article 107, 168; Chapter VII, 7, 19, 21, 88-95; "enemy states" clauses, 168, 172n.8; interpretation of, 25; and Security Council, 135-36
United Nations General Assembly: relationship with Security Council, 1-2, 5-7, 21; voting alignments in, viii-ix, 29-58
United Nations Security Council: abstention rate in voting, 82n.14; and Article 39 of UN Charter, 28n.17; changes in membership of, 141-47; China as member of, ix-x, 83-118; composition of, 137, 141-42, 153-54; efficiency of, 154-56, 162; equity as issue in, 20, 126-27, 153-54; feasibility of change in, 127-29, 166; and Germany, 144, 147, 157; informal consultations of, 8-9, 138; informal membership of, 136-39, 143-48; and Japan, 129-31, 157; military force as used by, 3-4, 5, 121-23; and military peacekeeping operations, 6-7, 121-23, 125; and Non-Aligned Movement, 136, 144-45, 147, 160, 165; nonpermanent membership of, 4-5, 8, 143, 159, 167, 172n.6; as open system, 136, 139-41; permanent membership of, 3, 137, 141-42, 156, 163-65; power as exercised by, 18-20; private meetings of, 8; procedures of, 7-9; proposals for reform of, vii, x-xi, 20, 120, 124-29, 166-69; reasons for reform of, 9-10, 20, 147-50; relationship with General Assembly, 1-2, 5-7, 21; representativeness of, 156-57; satisfaction versus power in, 66-69, 75; size of, 4, 8, 10, 65, 158, 163-64; structure and functions of, 1-5; and troop-contrib-

uting countries, 145-47; United States as powerful member of, 157-58; veto right of permanent members, xi, 2-3, 7, 10, 11n.1, 79-80, 127, 158-59, 165, 167-68, 172nn.4, 7; voting patterns of members, 52-54; voting power within, ix, 59-82, 128-29, 159-62; weaknesses of, 9
United States of America: China's attitude toward, 87-88, 104-5; power of in Security Council, 157-58; and use of military force by UN, 3-4
Uniting for Peace resolution (1950), 5-6, 80-81n.6
Universal Declaration of Human Rights, 22
Urquhart, Brian, 27n.2
USSR. *See* Union of Soviet Socialist Republics

veto power, xi, 2-3, 7, 10, 11n.1, 79-80, 127, 158-59, 165, 167-68, 172nn.4, 7
voting alignments in the General Assembly, viii-ix; and caucusing groups, 48-52; data analysis, 32-33, 56-57n.7, 57, nn.8, 9, 10; disarmament as issue in, 37-38, 47; issues underlying, 30-31, 55; patterns in, 39-48; political rights as issue in, 38-39, 51-52; among Security Council members, 52-54; self-determination as issue in, 33-38, 39-43, 51
voting blocs, 31, 69-70, 160-61

voting power in the Security Council, 59-82, 159-62; China's use of, ix-x, 83-84, 103-7; impact of continuing alliances on, 69-78; measurement of, 59-63; of non-veto members, 63-65, 75, 79; as tied to satisfaction, 66-69, 75; of veto members, 76-78, 79

Warsaw Pact countries, 31
Watson, Adam, 27n.6
White, N., 82n.14
Willson, Carolyn L., 150n.1
World Bank, 18; loan to China, 104
World Trade Organization, 106

Yemen, 61, 149, 162
Yoder, Karen, xii
Yugoslavia, 97, 102
Yugoslavia, former. *See* Bosnia-Herzegovina

Zacher, Mark, 27n.6
Zartman, I. William, 27n.7